PROSPERO'S ISLAND

Prospero, Duke of Milan, all 'rapt in secret studies' and 'neglecting worldly ends', loses his dukedom to his brother, Antonio, and is banished, with his baby daughter in a 'rotten carcase' of a boat on the open sea. In Shakespeare's play, which begins some twelve years later, Prospero, stranded on a desert island with the 'moon-calf' and 'monster', Caliban, a 'tricksy spirit' called Ariel and his now-grown daughter, Miranda, has become a master magician, a powerful magus who even wields control over the elements. *The Tempest* has puzzled and delighted audiences for nearly four centuries. What is the secret of Prospero's transformation? Noel Cobb sees this as the most important of all the riddles of the play. Using his own blend of methods involving history, alchemy, poetry and archetypal psychology, Cobb brings the issues so alive that the play seems to have been written yesterday.

What happens when you slip through the crack between the worlds and get a glimpse of the endlessly intricate web of interdependent origination? How do you return from the transcendental experience which has delightfully snatched you away from the depressing world of ordinary reality? How avoid the aversion to plunging back into the daily grind? How does spiritual reality come to have any point in our world? Does it matter? Cobb looks deeply into these questions and scries, within the crystal ball of Shakespeare's masterpiece, distinct archetypal patterns of gnosis behaving as actors in one of the most extraordinary dramas of all time. A drama about a shaman who has come through.

A book by a poet, traveller and psychotherapist about betrayal and exile, grief and despair, as well as courage and humility, magic and forgiveness.

Noel Cobb studied philosophy at the University of Michigan, then moved to Norway where he took a six year degree in psychology from the University of Oslo. In 1966 he came to England to study and work with Dr R. D. Laing and was a member of the Kingsley Hall Community in London's East End. With his wife, Fay, he has made expeditions to the Ahaggar mountains of the Algerian Sahara, North Afghanistan, Swat and the Himalayas of Nepal. In India he studied meditation under several masters of the Mahamudra tradition. Since 1975 he has resided in London where, after a Jungian training analysis, he now practises as a psychotherapist. During his seven years in Norway, he published four volumes of poetry and one novel in Norwegian, working with fellow poets on the translations. *Prospero's Island* is his first publication in Britain.

PROSPERO'S ISLAND

The Secret Alchemy at the Heart of
The Tempest

by

NOEL COBB

COVENTURE
23 Chesham Street, London SW1

Published 1984 by Coventure Limited,
23 Chesham Street, London SW1

Printed and bound in Great Britain by
Whitstable Litho Ltd., Whitstable, Kent

For Fay

1. **The sun needs the moon, like the cock needs the hen.**

O, Sun, you do not achieve anything alone, if I am not present
   with my forces,
   Just as the cock is useless without the help of the hen.
And in my turn I, the moon, want your help,
   Just as the cock is desired by the hen,
Foolish is he who would want to free from the bonds those things
   From which Nature urgently requires that they are united.

Acknowledgements

I would like to thank Linda Baer for writing from India to ask if I would send her a few lines on the meaning of life. I am especially indebted to Buntie Wills for her immeasurable warmth, down-to-earth wisdom and encouragement to write on *The Tempest*. Eternal thanks to the late Vajradhara Khamtrul Rinpoche, the VIIIth, for unceasingly pointing to the nature of mind. Thanks to Joseph Cobb, Robert Bly, Chogyam Trungpa Rinpoche and Ean Begg for their living examples. Thanks to Robert Beer for his incorrigible artistry and exquisite icons of celestial harmonies. Particular thanks to Geoffrey Blundell for giving Prospero a job. And a very special doff of the hat to the Guardian of the North Gate and Captain of the M/S "Zeus", Axel Jensen — a wordsmith whose pen illuminates the obscurity of the Baltic. Finally, no words can adequately express the appreciation I feel toward Fay, my wife, who has shared so many moments of heart's truth, from the labyrinths of Atakor to the yak-pastures of pure light.

For permission to use copyright material, the author gratefully makes the following acknowledgements to:

Routledge & Kegan Paul Plc for permission to quote from *The Collected Works of C. G. Jung*, and from his *Letters*, edited by Gerhard Adler (1973), Richard Wilhelm's *The I Ching or Book of Changes* (1951) and *John Dee — The World of an Elizabethan Magus* by Peter French (1972);

E. J. Brill of Leiden, for their permission to reproduce their English translation of the epigrams from *Atalanta Fugiens*;

A. D. Peters & Co. Ltd. for permission to quote from *Shakespeare's Last Plays* (1975) and *Giordano Bruno and the Hermetic Tradition* (1964), both by Dame Frances Yates;

Columbia University Press, for permission to quote from Heinrich Zimmer's *The King and the Corpse*;

Spring Publications, for permission to quote from *A Psychological*

Interpretation of the Golden Ass of Apuleius (1970) by Marie-Louise von Franz, *Jung's Psychological Types* by Marie-Louise von Franz and James Hillman and *Puer Papers* (1979) by James Hillman;

Princeton University Press, for permission to quote from *The Collected Works of C. G. Jung*, and from his *Letters*, edited by G. Adler and Richard Wilhelm's *The I Ching or Book of Changes*;

Pantheon Books, a division of Random House Inc., and R. D. Laing, for permission to quote from his book *Do You Love Me?*

The portrait of King James I of England is reproduced by permission of the National Maritime Museum, London, and the portrait of John Dee by courtesy of the Ashmolean Museum, Oxford.

Cover design: Robert Beer and Jutta Laing.

Contents

MUTUS LIBER, IN QUO TAMEN
tota *Philosophia herme-* *tica, figuris hieroglyphicis*
depingitur, ter optimo *maximo Deo misericordi*
consecratus, solisque *filiis artis dedicatus,*
authore cuius nomen *est Altus.*
21. ii. 82. Neg:
93. 82. 72. Neg:
82. xi. 33. Fued.

2.

Introduction:
The Making of a Magus

In England something happened to
thought between 1600 and 1610.[1]

but/ The art itself is nature.
— Wm. Shakespeare

The Tempest. What is it — if not the impeccable culmination of Shakespeare's
life-work, the final distillation of a theme which had occupied him since
the early production of *Love's Labour's Lost* (1594): the vital necessity of
earthiness as a counterbalance to intellect.

Shakespeare, like some strange Western incarnation of a Taoist sage,
walked a path which sought harmony between that which is above us and
that which is below. This is largely why he has come to represent, for our
culture, the ideal of wholeness, the complete individual.

In the Western world we have no vessel in which to contain our often
warring opposites except perhaps the little known *coniunctio* of the alchemists.
In our time there is a danger that the hemispheres will simply drift apart,
the *corpus callosum* of the psyche severed by the utilitarian knife of 'scientific
objectivity'. It regularly appears that the right hand does not even wish
to know what the left may be doing, and the left is frequently paralyzed
by the crimes the right commits. Both Light and Dark ignore the common
ground of twilight. The Above and Below co-exist in a seething state of
embittered estrangement. On some level to a greater or lesser degree we
are all aware of this.

The time of *The Tempest* is the time of the Golden Age of Alchemy.
Alchemical images permeate the play. They flash and fulminate through
its pages like gleaming droplets of quicksilver caught in the fusty folds of
an alchemist's cloak.

The strange thing is that these images are still valid today. And how we need symbols of reconciliation.

Prospero, as the image-quickening magus of Imagination, belongs to all humanity. He is ours — as the archetypal figure of the shaman-who-has-come-through: Merlin released from the eternal thicket of his spells. The spirit at last at rest in the arms of the soul.

Spirit and soul. I use these terms advisedly, for they mark out the extremities in the imaginal territory of this musing. Thanks to the work of C. G. Jung and, more recently, that of the American analyst, James Hillman, it is now possible to distinguish spirit and soul and to bring soul back to psychology.

In a remarkable paper called *Peaks and Vales — The Soul/Spirit Distinction as a Basis for the Differences between Psychotherapy and Spiritual Discipline,* Hillman poetically depicts the two visions of soul and spirit.[2] He shows how spirit aims for the peaks and the peak-experiences, while soul pulls us to the depths where we travail in the vale of troubles. Spirit is brilliant and dazzling, fiery and piercing. It is masculine intellect, logos, in its purest aspect. Whereas soul is moist, dark and alive with feeling — the essence of feminine relatedness. The spirit is an arrow of light, speeding ever higher through ascending circles of infinite intelligence. The soul is all that is near and dear, painful and poignant. It is also like the image-play of reflections in a bottomless forest lake. Our lives are the resonance of the music spun from those two cosmic principles of Earth and Sky: the soil and water of soul, the fire and air of spirit.

From the point of view of spirit, soul lacks discipline and rigour. It is all dream and fantasy, brooding and musing. The spirit is tempted to abandon soul altogether or subject it to Herculean labours. This can easily become repression. And for the past twelve centuries this has largely been the case.

Hillman places the date of the soul's loss of its dominion as 787 A.D. — the date of the Church Council at Nicea — when images were deprived of their inherent authenticity. To counter this he calls for a return to a listening to the speech of the soul: images. To me this is the most important single contribution to psychology in the twentieth century. Of course, he shares this contribution with Jung, who first stated it, though — and this is important for all of us who think in English — Hillman speaks a much more graceful and imaginative language than even the best translations of Jung.

Parallel to the general misogyny traditional in Western culture and the artificial (masculine) definition of feminine inferiority, there is an obvious imbalance in the way Western culture has valued soul and spirit. The devaluation of soul has been with us for a long time.

In Shakespeare's time the attacks on the soul had not finally driven it into exile, though over a century of witch-hunts had been preparing the way for the soul-withering breath of the fiery spirit of scientific-rationalism and the coming age of 'enlightenment'. It is not necessary, perhaps, to state the obvious: that Shakespeare was a man of extraordinary vision and perspective. His plays are not only timeless, they show a profound, almost obsessed interest in history, but not in any usual fashion; more as an observer of natural history might look at human happenings. For Shakespeare, man's history was not separate from nature.

I feel that Shakespeare can help us immensely in our revisioning of the soul-spirit polarity. In particular, he shows us how interdependent these two are. There is an implicit emphasis on their 'dual unity' — as though he were using this as a method for the examination and articulation of a hidden but fundamental structure of psychic reality.

Coleridge makes the startling observation that in the voice of the bard nature itself seems to be speaking: [3]

> Nature, the prime genial artist, inexhaustible in diverse powers, is equally inexhaustible in forms . . . and even such is the appropriate excellence of her chosen poet, of our own Shakespeare, — himself a nature humanized, a genial understanding directing self-consciously a power and an implicit wisdom deeper even than our consciousness.

How Shakespeare understood the relationship between art and nature can be understood from lines like these from *The Winter's Tale*. In Polixenes' words:

> Yet nature is made better by no mean
> But nature makes that mean: so, over that art
> Which you say adds to nature, is an art
> That nature makes . . . this is an art
> Which does mend nature — change it rather; but
> The art itself is nature.
>
> (IV.4. 89-97)

The art of the play as the play of the art. What extraordinary poetics of qualities! A poetry *and* a phenomenology: qualities of the elements, qualities of fate, qualities of character, qualities of truth, and through it all: the qualities of the isle. And these qualities not seen simply in isolated juxtaposition, but intermingling in a subtle dance of secret symmetry.

Even so, we must make a leap of creative imagination if this "implicit wisdom deeper than our consciousness" is to become an integral part of our psyches. The magus himself in the epilogue of this, the bard's most

magical play, pleads with us to use our imagination to free him and not
abandon him on that "bare island":

> But release me from my bands
> With the help of your good hands:
> Gentle breath of yours my sails
> Must fill, or else my project fails . . .

What does he mean? Must we accept the simple-minded literal
interpretation that he is just the actor asking for applause? Is Prospero not
rather asking to be allowed to live in history, within us? I believe so. Not
cut off from the mainland, but reinstated in his rightful place as Wise Old
Man in the kingdom of the self.

Our way into an understanding of the play will be through its images.
And here we come up against strong prejudice against our method.

> The hatred of the image, the fear of its power, and of the imagination,
> is very old and very deep in our culture. [4]

Whereas, if we respond to Prospero/Shakespeare's appeal to experience
The Tempest imaginatively, we enter into the spirit and soul of the play with
a delight in the image, a love of the imagination and a respect for its power.
Only then will the mute hieroglyphs begin to sing.

In Elizabethan England, just as in the past two decades of our own century,
there was a great proliferation of occult and esoteric teachings. Then, during
the reign of King James I (from the "barbarous North" as one modern
scholar puts it) a reaction set in. Anyone reading King James' treatises on
demonology and witchcraft can see that here was a man who *believed* that
certain "ungodly creatures" could, through the aid of familiar spirits and
wicked practices, "suddenly cause to be brought unto them, all kindes of
daintie disshes", "(bring) Wine out of a Wall", "cure or cast on disease",
cause men to be impotent, create madness, kill at a distance and raise storms
by magic. [5] In fact, he considered it to be a sin against God *not* to believe
that such things existed.

His zeal in torturing those suspected of witchcraft was unbounded. So
assured in his Divine Right, he expressed not the slightest doubt in the
complicity of one Dr John Fian and proceeded to have all his fingernails
"riven and pulled off with an instrument called in Scottish a *Turkas*, which
in England wee call a payre of pincers, and vnder euerie nayle there was
thrust in two needles ouer euen up to the heads". He notes that the Doctor
"neuer shronke anie whit" and since he had retracted an earlier confession
(made under torture), the King caused him to be put back into the "bootes",
which so crushed his legs "that the bloud and marrowe spouted forth in

3. **Portrait of James I of England, 1610.**

great abundance, whereby they were made unseruiceable for euer." James then notes that "notwithstanding al these grieuous paines and cruell torments hee would not confesse anie thing, so deeply had the deuill entered his heart."[6] Unable to get a clear confession that Fian was consorting with the devil and had helped raise the tempest that nearly sank his ship (on its return voyage from Oslo where he had married Queen Anne), James sentenced Fian, had him put in a cart and strangled and his body thrown on a pyre. This was the king for whom *The Tempest* was first performed.

In his advocation of the use of torture to extract the confession of the witch, James sounds a note which was repeated in the first formulations of what came to be the modern scientific method of torturing nature in order to discover 'her' secrets, as devised by his, and Shakespeare's contemporary, Francis Bacon.[7]

Quite a good cause can be made, as Dame Frances Yates has done in her delightful book, *Shakespeare's Last Plays*, for the thesis that with the figure of Prospero, Shakespeare was actually defending the controversial magus, John Dee, and with him, indirectly, the whole magico-scientific tradition, loosely called 'Rosicrucianism' by Frances Yates, which Dee had exemplified in his lifetime (1527-1608).

> Now, if the first version of *The Tempest* appeared around 1611, the date at which Shakespeare chose to glorify a Dee-like magus is significant. For Dee had fallen into deep disfavour after his return from his mysterious continental mission in 1589, and he was completely cast off by James I after his accession. When the old Elizabethan magus appealed to James in 1604 for help in clearing his reputation from charges of conjuring devils, James would have nothing to do with him, in spite of his earnest protests that his art and science were good and virtuous and that he had no commerce with evil spirits. The old man to whose scientific learning the Elizabethan age had been so deeply indebted was disgraced in the reign of James and died in great poverty in 1608.[8]

John Dee's banishment from royal favour is certainly symbolic of an important change in collective attitudes towards the occult philosophy, and I am certain that Frances Yates is right to emphasize this. And no-one, reading *The Tempest*, can miss the central importance of Prospero's own banishment. The painful poetry of rejection pulses through the play like a deep and open wound. The fate of Dee under the reign of James must have resonated throughout the whole of the English psyche. Obviously, Shakespeare, like any sensitive and passionate artist, would have been concerned. Frances Yates, however, goes so far as to suggest in a more recent book[9] that Dee was even the model for Lear, who was also the victim of base ingratitude. I am not sure I can follow her in this. As I hope to show in this study there

4. **Portrait of John Dee, 1594.**

is a wisdom in the plays quite apart from the defence of a tradition, and there is a danger that this can be obscured by the excitement of discovering in the distant past antecedents to one's current mythic fantasy. I am aware that I am not immune to this process, and that is why I stick with the text. I am grateful to Frances Yates for the scholarly insights into Shakespeare's England which she has given us, but there is also a need to fathom the psychological complexities of the bard's work and to listen to what he has to say about the shadow side of things. He does not simply justify Prospero/Dee as being a victim of evil-minded men and innocent of any complicity in the disaster which befalls him. Shakespeare did not see the problem in such easy black-and-white contrasts, but full of subtle shades of colour. Dee had his dark side, just as James had his light. I think Frances Yates is right, however, in calling our attention to the obvious *ferment* of the time with regard to the moral status of the magical arts like alchemy, astrology, scrying, conjuring, spell-binding and loosening, healing and divination.

At what a pitch this controversy over the authenticity and validity of the occult teachings was raging, we can understand better by comparing Ben Jonson's *The Alchemist* with Shakespeare's play. Jonson's piece is a harsh satire in which the central character, a student of the occult sciences, is presented as a charlatan and a cheat. The play satirises alchemy, mathematics and mathematical magic, the conjuring of spirits, Paracelsian medicine and 'Rosicrucianism' itself. The central character, Subtle, is obviously a parody of John Dee. The play was first performed in 1610, a year before the earliest known performance of *The Tempest*, by The King's Men. Everything which is noble and profound in *The Tempest* is wittily ridiculed in *The Alchemist*. It is apparent that Shakespeare and Jonson saw things very differently. Frances Yates says: [10]

> To define the opposition as Protestant versus Catholic would be a misleading and much too narrow interpretation. On the one hand there is a 'Rosicrucian' type of culture, inheriting the traditions of Renaissance magic as expanded by alchemical and Paracelsist influence, an esoteric approach to religion involving tolerant and kindly attitudes to religious differences, and a hope of reconciliation through the younger generation. This is Shakespeare in *The Tempest* and in the Last Plays generally. On the other hand, there is dislike and contempt for all such influences. This is Jonson in *The Alchemist*.

> Or, if one thinks of the attitudes in both plays to the type of 'occult philosophy' taught by Agrippa, Shakespeare in *The Tempest* makes a positive use of this, to deepen and expand religious consciousness through a magical approach reaching into what is vaguely called the esoteric sphere. For Jonson, this is anathema, and all 'occult philosophy' is a cheat and a delusion.

Jonson was an intelligent man. He also knew a fair amount of the 'Rosicrucian' literature, which is obvious from the use of the terminology in *The Alchemist*. That he had much actual experience of the 'magical practices' he condemns so out of hand is a matter of conjecture, though I would strongly doubt it. His view is that of cynicism and rational scepticism. He had no sympathy for those who were seriously committed to the Art. This attitude is echoed in our day by many critics of 'religion', from Freud to Marx.

Eventually, and how appropriately, all that was previously rejected and devalued can be revealed as a powerful source of inspiration, instruction and strength. Where before, there was only a conceptualized understanding and a constricted empathy, there is now an abundance, an overflowing of love and wisdom. The adept crosses the threshold. He becomes a master. And because he prospers, all who come into his presence prosper. This I feel is the true significance of Prospero and his vicissitudes. As it is said in the great Emerald Tablet of Hermes Trismegistus so often referred to by the alchemists:

WHAT IS BELOW
IS LIKE WHAT IS
ABOVE —
THAT THE MIRACLE
OF THE ONE THING
MAY BE ACCOMPLISHED

5.

PART I
THE ISLAND

PART 1

THE ISLAND

1. The Tempest

6. **The wind carried him in its belly.**

Thunder repeated: the image of SHOCK.
Thus in fear and trembling
The superior man sets his life in order
And examines himself![1]

We cannot call her winds and waters sighs
and tears; they are greater storms and
tempests than almanacs can report![2]

The Tempest opens in an absolutely exuberant burst of wild energy. Barely contained within its form, the energy seems to be trying to leap out of itself in a way which is reminiscent of those passages in Beethoven's last quartets when one no longer knows precisely what emotion is being expressed. Could it be terror, exaltation, unbounded grief, the sound of the soul at its outermost extremity, or is it the final rending apart of the cocoon before the butterfly of psyche unfolds its wings and bursts free? Whatever else, we are aware of the highest pitch of turmoil. In the midst of a "tempestuous noise of thunder and lightning" a ship's captain calls for his bo'sun to get the crew immediately to work to save the boat from running aground or capsizing. In a matter of seconds we are transported to the heart of a raging storm. And thus begins the subtle enchantment of this most mysterious and magical of all Shakespeare's plays.

It is a storm to end all storms. Everything accentuates the exigency of the moment. On deck we see the figure of the bo'sun, running back and forth, directing his mates to take in the topsail. Despite his brief appearance in the play the bo'sun creates a powerful impression because he is the symbol of fearless, practical intelligence in the face of crisis.

And *crisis* it certainly is — though this knowledge has not yet penetrated, it seems, into the awareness of the passengers: four royal personages and their attendants, staggering over the deck in their luxurious robes, importuning the bo'sun as to the whereabouts of the master.

These men represent a special type of ignorance, which can be very intelligent as well, cleverly turning a blind eye to what is really going on; refusing to see the signs of impending crisis. The bo'sun's answer is a whipcrack:

> Do you not hear him? You mar our labour: keep your cabins: you do
> assist the storm.

(I.i.13-14)

The nobles' authority holds no sway — they are awkward obstructions, merely in the way. As the boatswain says, "What cares these roarers for the name of king?" (I.i.16)

The distinction between true authority, which rests on an actual command of the elements and a simulated one, which is revealed to be at the mercy of them, is further emphasized by the bo'sun's words to Gonzalo, who, Shakespeare informs us in the *Dramatic Personae* is "an honest old counsellor".

> You are a counsellor; if you can command these elements to silence,
> and work the peace of the presence, we will not hand a rope more; use
> your authority: if you cannot, give thanks you have lived so long, and
> make yourself ready in your cabin for the mischance of the hour, if it
> so hap. Cheerly, good hearts! Out of our way, I say.

(I.i.20-27)

Devastating plain talk to an honest old counsellor. And yet, how necessary! It calls to mind the increasing number of people who would nowadays call themselves analysts, therapists, psychiatrists and so on, who, in spite of all their good intentions, have no command of the language of silence and who cannot "work the peace of the presence".

An eminent psychiatrist may be able to fool everyone at the clinic where he is king, but his family see another reality. As R. D. Laing puts it in his wry *Song of the false guru's wife*:

> If only it were as easy
> as they try to make it sound

I'd always be chirpy and cheery
   and whirl round and round and round
   and whirl round and round and round
     But
     his Chakras are filled up with sawdust
     his Kundalini is coiled up in glue
     his third eye is stuffed with broken glass
     and I don't know what to do[13]

Strangely, Gonzalo muses that he has "great comfort from this fellow" (I.i.28), and, in spite of feeling struck by the bo'sun's unsentimental observation, he admits the reality of his situation. In a tortured and contorted image he confesses that his fate is not in his own hands. It is, for better or for worse, actually tied up with the bo'sun's!

> . . .methinks he hath no drowning mark upon him; his complexion is perfect gallows. Stand fast, good Fate, to his hanging: make the rope of his destiny our cable, for our own doth little advantage. If he be not born to be hanged, our case is miserable.
>
>   (I.i.28-33)

Gonzalo's fellow passengers seem even more estranged from the situation. They wander about the deck helplessly arrogant, and rather foolish, given the mood of imminent catastrophe. The bo'sun treats them like children:

> Yet again! what do you here? Shall we give o'er, and drown? Have you a mind to sink?
>
>   (I.i.38-39)

Sebastian, brother of Alonso, King of Naples, screams a hysterical curse at the bo'sun:

> A pox o' your throat, you bawling, blasphemous, incharitable dog!
>
>   (I.i.40)

But the boatswain does not react to Sebastian's spiteful jabs. An awareness of the true situation dissolves any need for self-justification. He simply shouts back: "Work you, then!"

When Antonio, Duke of Milan, adds his curses to those of Sebastian, claiming that they (the nobles) are less afraid of drowning than the bo'sun, we begin to wonder. Who is the true nobility here? The conceited, powerless, cursing royalty or the level-headed, pragmatic bo'sun, grappling with powers far greater than himself? Gonzalo, truly alarmed at his compatriots' lack of awareness and their self-indulgent abuse of 'authority', utters a disguised defence of the bo'sun:

I'll warrant him for drowning,[14] though the ship were no stronger than
a nutshell, and as leaky as an unstanched wench.

(I.i.46-48)

So deeply is Gonzalo animated by the turbulence without and within
that his images spring with a startling clarity out of the depths of the psyche.
We are told, if we are listening, something very important about Gonzalo's
function in the play. A leaking boat is a danger because the sea can enter
it and cause it to sink. An "unstanched wench" is a woman who is losing
menstrual blood. It is strange connection that has occurred in Gonzalo's
unconscious. It tells us that Gonzalo is somehow more connected with the
feminine, perhaps slightly more at home with it, than his fellows.

Note the fact that the *Dramatis Personae* for *The Tempest* lists *only one* female
part, except for the mythical personages who appear in the masque. In this
first scene the feminine is most conspicuous by its absence. This imbalance
is pertinent to the whole structure of the play. In another sense the feminine
is, however, very much present in the image of the sea, that vast unknown
which surrounds the whole play from beginning to end. If, following Jung,
we consider the sea to be the psychological symbol of the unconscious and
that itself to be feminine, then the sense of the storm becomes clearer. The
tiny boat with its masculine company, from the mainland, i.e., the civilization
built up through man's conscious efforts, represents the limited realm of
ego-consciousness. The swelling, life-and-death giving, unfathomable ocean
represents the realm of the matrix of consciousness, the unconscious source
and origin. The storm, this convulsive upheaval, a *grand mal* seizure of wind
and waves, is thus an enactment on the macrocosmic level of a far-reaching
and violent *enantiodromia*[15] within psyche itself. It is emblematic for the whole
play: it sets the stage for what is to follow. This storm is no accident. It
has the same numinous and mythical overtones as the famous storm which
pursued Jonah when he was fleeing "the presence of the Lord":[16]

> But the Lord sent out a great wind into the sea, and there was a mighty
> tempest in the sea, so that the ship was like to be broken.

Neither nobility, fearless intelligence nor honest counsel can calm this
storm. As it seems inevitable that the ship will not clear the rocky coast,
the mariners cry for mercy and shout farewells to their wives and children.
King Alonso and his son, Ferdinand, are "at prayers" and Gonzalo expresses
a wish to assist them, but Sebastian and Antonio blame the disaster on the
crew and continue ranting. At the end of the scene, Gonzalo invokes dry
land with great longing:

Now would I give a thousand furlongs of sea for an acre of barren ground,
long heath, broom, furze, anything. The wills above be done! but I would
fain die a dry death.

(I.i.64-67)

Sebastian and Antonio represent that relentlessly rational kind of
masculine intellect which scoffs at anything outside the empirical. Theirs
is the standpoint of literalism.[17] They are the cold and ruthless, shadow-
aspects of Logos in its most arrogant and one-sided form. The others of
the company are less fanatical. Alonso and his son are actually praying —
a highly non-rational activity. And Gonzalo, who stands between them,
involes a *plurality* of divine powers, thereby demonstrating that he does not
properly belong in the society of atheists or Christian monotheists. Thus,
he also represents a connection with an older, archaic part of the psyche,
harking back to pre-Christian times.

The tempest thus understood is a tremendous psychological crisis brought
about by an over-evaluation of the (masculine) intellect. All this uproar,
human and non-human, perfectly expresses what Jung called ''the passionate
emotionality that precedes the recognition of unconscious contents.'' (CW
14.p.295)

2. The Island

7. **The king, swimming in the sea, calling in a loud voice: He who saves
   me will get a tremendous reward.**

**In the sea of the unconscious the island represents a
split-off portion of the conscious psyche (as we know,
beneath the sea, islands are usually connected with the
mainland), and here the island represents an autonomous
complex, quite apart from the ego, with a kind of
intelligence of its own.**[8]

Even though Marie-Louise von Franz, in the above quotation, is speaking
of a Norwegian fairy tale, her insight applies equally to *The Tempest*. Here,
we are engaged in taking a step out of the cut-and-dried approach of literalism
and into the realm of the imagination, where we shall try to apprehend the
meaning of the play on its own ground — that of the imagination, thus
creating a playground for fantasy, a place for it to play with the play. The
ship, the sea, the storm, the island and all the players are, therefore, not
confined within the cage of literal meaning. We are free to see them as images
conjured by Shakespeare's imagination in response to a contemporary attack
on the whole validity of spiritual practice.

The scene we have before us is "an uninhabited island" — a strange
designation considering that it is peopled. An old man and a young girl
stand in front of a cave opening, somehow above and outside the storm,
intensely discussing it. The girl, Miranda, is pleading with her father,

Prospero, to have pity on the men whom she assumes must be suffering in the tempest, created, she suspects, by her father's "Art".

> If by your Art, my dearest father, you have
> Put the wild waters in this roar, allay them.
> The sky, it seems, would pour down stinking pitch,
> But that the sea, mounting to the welkin's cheek,
> Dashes the fire out. O, I have suffered
> With those that I saw suffer! a brave vessel,
> (Who had, no doubt, some noble creature in her,)
> Dash'd all to pieces. O, the cry did knock
> Against my very heart! Poor souls, they perish'd!
> Had I been any god of power, I would
> Have sunk the sea within the earth, or ere
> It should the good ship so have swallowed, and
> The fraughting souls within her.

                                                          (I.ii.1-13)

What is most essential in this first speech of Miranda's is her moved and moving awareness of suffering. She feels the agony of the souls in distress knocking against her "very heart". I feel that this profound identification with the "souls" on the boat leaves no doubt as to her own identity as the carrier of soul in the play.[19]

Prospero's words in answer fall like the gentle words of Christ calming his distraught disciples:

> *Pros.*   Be collected:
> No more amazement: tell your piteous heart
> There's no harm done.
>
> *Mir.*   O woe the day!
>
> *Pros.*   No harm.
> I have done nothing but in care of thee,
> Of thee, my dear one; thee, my daughter, who
> Art ignorant of what thou art; nought knowing
> Of whence I am, nor that I am more better
> Than Prospero, master of a full poor cell,
> And thy no greater father.

                                                          (I.ii.14-21)

Prospero tells his daughter to wipe her eyes and have comfort, assuring her that he has had no evil intentions toward the souls on the ship and has even miraculously ensured that not the slightest harm has come to them:

The direful spectacle of the wreck; which touch'd
The very virtue of compassion in thee,
I have with such provision in my Art
So safely ordered, that there is no soul —
No, not so much perdition as an hair
Betid to any creature in the vessel
Which thou heard'st cry, which thou saw'st sink.

                                                        (I.ii.26-32)

    We now understand that the tempest has been Prospero's doing, though
we do not yet know why. But everything in Prospero's manner inspires
us with a confidence that he is motivated by benevolence and that he is aware
of a higher meaning in the storm than any the ship's passengers could know.
How true this is with our own shipwrecks, disasters and breakdowns in life!
How often we deny them any higher meaning, swearing and cursing our
fate or giving way to panic or despair. Yet, if we could but hear that still,
small voice in the centre of the storm, we might perhaps discover that our
disasters were potential gateways into higher, and deeper, levels of meaning
in our lives.

3. A Tale to Cure Deafness

8. If you kill one of the four, everybody will be dead immediately.

Interwoven in Prospero's speeches of reassurance is another theme: the past and the story of who he and his daughter are. I cannot emphasize this point enough: that this theme is what gives the play weight and substance and transforms it into a true alchemical teaching. So much so, that improvising on Caliban (who is shortly to appear), we can say that *The Tempest* as far surpasseth all dubious esoteric treatises "as great does least". It is what makes it a masterpiece and a work which so many have praised in the highest words, often without even fully understanding why it has moved them. As one Shakespearean scholar has claimed:[20]

> *The Tempest* is thus at the same time the most perfect work of art and the most crystal act of mystic vision in our literature.

In conjunction with what I said earlier about the tendency of spirit to soar up on out of sight of the depths and to neglect soul, becoming an imbalanced, one-sided affair, I would like to suggest that in this play Shakespeare is primarily interested in the cultivation of soul — as psychological understanding.[21] And when soul has reached her maturity, come of age as it were, she can then merge with spirit in a happy *hieros gamos*, or sacred marriage. But we are jumping ahead. First, let us hear Prospero's story:

Pros.   The hour's now come;
          The very minute bids thee ope thine ear;
          Obey, and be attentive. Canst thou remember
          A time before we came unto this cell?
          I do not think thou canst, for then thou wast not
          Out three years old.

Mir.   Certainly, sir, I can.

Pros.   By what? by any other house or person?
          Of any thing the image tell me, that
          Hath kept with thy remembrance.

Mir.   'Tis far off,
          And rather like a dream than an assurance
          That my remembrance warrants. Had I not
          Four or five women once that tended me?

                                              (I.ii.37-47)

As Prospero begins to speak to Miranda about their past, he takes off his magic garment and lays it down. The mantle, a symbol of his Art, is thus more like a mask than an emblem of his true self. It refers to his role as magician and wizard-priest, masculine manifestations related to the realm of spirit. To relate authentically with Miranda, however, and thus to his soul, Prospero must drop that identification and step out of the realm of the spirit. He then talks to her directly and simply, as a kind father would do.

Miranda remembers very little of her life before the island — except that four or five women once tended her. However, this one memory is significant. It further connects her with the feminine and, in particular, with the world of tending, caring.

Prospero now explains that they came to the island some twelve years before and that previous to that time he was the Duke of Milan, a "prince of power". The only mention of Prospero's wife, Miranda's mother, is when Prospero says: "Thy mother was a piece of virtue" (I.ii.56). Nothing more is said. We have no other image of her. There is no explanation of what happened to her or why she did not accompany them to the island. I feel that this further underscores the psychological reality of Miranda as a carrier of soul — she reflects Prospero's own inner deepening, his growing awareness of the world as "the vale of soul-making".[22]

Now, we, and Miranda, hear the history which led up to their arrival on the island:

Pros.   My brother, and thy uncle, call'd Antonio, —
          I pray thee, mark me, that a brother should
          Be so perfidious! — he whom next thyself

Of all the world I lov'd, and to him put
The manage of my state; as at that time
Through all the signories it was the first,
And Prospero the prime duke, being so reputed
In dignity, and for the liberal Arts
Without a parallel; those being all my study,
The government I cast upon my brother,
And to my state grew stranger, being transported
And rapt in secret studies.

(I.ii.66-67)

Prospero goes on to tell how his brother gradually usurped control of the dukedom and "having both the key/ Of officer and office, set all hearts i' th' state/ To what tune pleas'd his ear . . ." (I.ii.83-85). He likens his brother to ivy and himself to a "princely trunk" which the ivy hid and from which it sucked away the "verdure" (strength, vitality). Here, we have a ruler, a "prime duke", who was "reputed in dignity" and without a parallel in the liberal Arts, who actually abandons the affairs of state because he is so "transported and rapt in secret studies". Given the ambiguity in "my state", we can also say that "And to my state grew stranger" also implies that he grew estranged from himself. It is in this estranged state that he allows his brother to take his place as ruler of the land. Despite the botanical inaccuracy of the ivy image,[23] it is a powerful symbol for the loss of power — sinister in its vampire-like overtones.

Superficially, we might condemn Antonio, but if we meditate on the relationship between the two brothers, we will discover a hidden affinity. It is almost as if they were polarized aspects of the same psyche. The more Prospero turns toward the realm of logos, the spirit and the intellect, and, consequently away from the world, the more Antonio gains in substance, power and energy. Antonio's power is thus directly related to Prospero's unconsciousness of the situation. In Jung's words:[24]

> Our unconscious bounds our field of vision and that is the reason why the shadow becomes the symbol of the unconscious of man.

Antonio is a perfect screen for Prospero's unconscious projections. He is, in more ways than one, Prospero's shadow. In the next lines Shakespeare paints an incredibly subtle picture of the intricate dance between the two.

Pros.   I pray thee, mark me.
I, thus neglecting worldly ends, all dedicated
To closeness and the bettering of my mind
With that which, but by being so retir'd,
O'er-prized all popular rate, in my false brother

> Awak'd an evil nature; and my trust,
> Like a good parent, did beget of him
> A falsehood in its contrary, as great
> As my trust was; which had indeed no limit,
> A confidence sans bound. He being thus lorded,
> Not only with what my revenue yielded,
> But what my power might else exact, like one
> Who having into truth, by telling of it,
> Made such a sinner of his memory,
> To credit his own lie, he did believe
> He was indeed the duke; out o' th' substitution,
> And executing th' outward face of royalty,
> With all prerogative; — hence his ambition growing —
> Dost thou hear?

Mir.   Your tale, sir, would cure deafness.

Pros.   To have no screen between this part he played
> And him he played it for, he needs will be
> Absolute Milan. Me, poor man, my library
> Was dukedom large enough . . .

                                                        (I.ii.89-110)

The picture we are getting of Prospero at this time is one of a man totally dedicated to the intellect and the realm of the spirit. He wishes to "better his mind" — a noble aim — but he is aiming at the perfection of a single aspect. "Neglecting worldly ends", he loses touch with those functions necessary to wholeness and completeness. Gazing at the far-distant, celestial realms of enlightenment, he loses cognisance of what is happening in his own house, virtually underneath his nose: the fact that his brother-shadow has taken over the rulership of the dukedom and plans to displace him.

This fascination of the spiritual/intellectual reflects a rather masculine preoccupation and one which has deep roots in Western culture. I am reminded of Faust's speech outside the City Gate, where he gives vent to his longings to fly like a god with the sun away from the earth and drink "streams of quenchless light", leaving the night far behind.[25] We are familiar with this tendency within Christianity — where people want to leave the world and become absorbed in God. It is also present in Buddhism when people assume that *Nirvana* is something totally separate from *Samsara*, positing a state outside and antithetical to the world. The ancient Mahasiddhas of India constantly tried to correct this view:[26]

> There is not the slightest difference of Samsara from Nirvana,
> Nor is there the slightest difference of Nirvana from Samsara.

That which is the limit of Nirvana is also the limit of Samsara.
In between them not the slightest shade of difference is found.

Jung may have been thinking of Faust when he wrote the following words
in 1954:

> "Spirit" always seems to come from above, while from below comes
> everything that is sordid and worthless. For people who think in this
> way, spirit means highest freedom, a soaring over the depths, deliverance
> from the prison of the chthonic world, and hence a refuge for all those
> timorous souls who do not want to become anything different.
>
> (CW.9.i.19)

In our own time the great expansion of consciousness in the 1960's through
the use of agents like lysergic acid resulted, for many, in a disgust for 'the
world' and an aversion to dirtying one's (spiritual) hands with mundane
realities. Perhaps only now are the drop-outs from that generation becoming
aware of the shadow aspect of this resignation: a vast, amorphous darkness
in the form of a growing bureaucratic, serialized State machinery, ravenously
gorging itself on the power which all the separate individuals abandoned
in their flight from Society, Establishment and Authority.

My feeling about *The Tempest* is that Shakespeare was aware of a similar
constellation of opposites in his own time. Prospero, as I pointed out in
the introduction, has been identified by modern researchers as an exemplary
model of the Renaissance magus, with close affinities to the historical
personage, John Dee.

At this point it is illuminating to look at the figure of Dee and the world-
view of the magus in Shakespeare's time. It is impossible to go into great
detail, but a general knowledge of this aspect is essential to an understanding
of the problem which had gripped Shakespeare's imagination.

According to Frances Yates, "John Dee (1527-1608) was a genuine
mathematician of considerable importance, intensely interested in all
mathematical studies and in the application of mathematics to produce results
in applied sciences."[27] He was a favourite of Queen Elizabeth, who greatly
encouraged and supported him during her reign. He acted as court astrologer
and certainly, for a select few, as a kind of hierophant of the hermetico-
religious tradition in the line of Agrippa and Ficino. He was an expert
geographer and engineer and a consultant on problems of navigation. He
was the teacher of men like Philip Sydney, thereby wielding an enormous
influence over the development of the hermetic way of thinking in England.

Dee believed that mathematics was a key to understanding the universe
and, like Pico della Mirandola, that "by numbers, a way is had, to the
searching out, and understanding of every thing able to be known".[28] He

was a close student of Agrippa's occult philosophy — in particular, the practice of angel-summoning. He distinguished between a practical mathematics ("the useful wax") and a mystical mathematics ("the delightful honey") which the philosopher (the "Bee") could gather. Ultimately, he believed that all things have their being in numbers: [29]

> Objects or creatures exist because they were created (numbered) with what might be termed idea-numbers, or form-numbers, in the mind of God; the form-numbers can be equated with the mathematical formulae that describe things as they are in reality. If the form-number of a certain item becomes lacking in the mind of God, however, that item will be 'discreated'. If the form number of the toad were forgotten, for example, all toads would cease to exist. According to *magia*, the discovery of the form-number that signifies a particular thing gives man power over that thing, just as formulae, according to modern science, gives man power over his surroundings.

This description, dry as it sounds, is an extraordinary crystallization of — in Jung's terms — a highly introverted thinking and intuitive function. Number and ratio have become the lens through which the individual sees everything. The evaluation of experience through the feeling function and the concrete perception of objects in the sensual field have both been undervalued and left uncultivated.

This overemphasis on the masculine intelligence, the intellect, comes out even more clearly in the following passage, where Peter French is describing Dee's relation to Agrippa — who stood behind Dee and much of the hermetico-religious tradition of the Renaissance.

> Agrippa unequivocally says that the key to operation in the angelic realm is 'the dignifying of men to this so sublime vertue and power'. Only the intellect, the highest faculty of the soul, can work the wonders connected with this level of magical operations. Agrippa gives a detailed formula for attaining a Hermetic gnosis, which is basic to all religious magic. The magus attains proper 'dignification' by two steps. The first, in which he leaves 'carnal affections, fragile sense and the materiall passions', leads to the second, which is the gnostic ascent through the three worlds 'to an intellect pure & conjoyned with the power of the gods'. In his fullest dignity the religious magus must perform various ceremonies, expiations, consecrations and holy rites. The end result of all this is that his mind will become 'pure and divine, inflamed with a religious love, adorned with hope, directed by faith, placed in the hight and top of the humane soul'. At his heights, the religious magus could theoretically change the stars and control the heavenly powers. *But the strain would be so great that his body would soon be destroyed and his spiritual*

essence would be completely absorbed into the Godhead. This transformation was exactly what Dee was attempting to achieve through his magic.[30] (Italics mine)

I feel that Shakespeare, with much sympathy for the quest of the magus, was very aware of the shadow side of such a project and that he attempted in *The Tempest* to give it his blessing *but* — with the profundity of his understanding of balance and wholeness — he has demonstrated how this endeavour must be carried out in order to arrive at its greatest fulfilment. The reason why *The Tempest* is the greatest mystery play of our tradition, in contrast with Ben Johnson's *The Alchemist*, which remains on the level of a witty satire, is that Shakespeare understood the truth of alchemy as being a transmutation of man's *prima materia*, his basic nature, into the pure gold of the self. The fact that the world was full of imposters and charlatans, crackpots and spiritual con-men did not blind him to the fact that the true path actually existed. This true path was considerably more arduous than popular conception would have it.

John Dee was an important and controversial figure during most of Shakespeare's lifetime. As I mentioned earlier, he fell from royal favour during the reign of King James and died in poverty in 1608. Even if Shakespeare did not know him personally, he must certainly have heard much about him. There would, however, have been no lack of contemporary figures on which to model the initial character of Prospero. Shakespeare must have been aware of the disturbing events in the life of Rudolf II (1552-1612), the eccentric and introverted Holy Roman Emperor whom Dee visited in Prague (1584) in a bid to become the Emperor's resident philosopher and mathematician. Like Prospero, Rudolf lived in seclusion, dabbling in the arts and sciences while his kingdom slowly disintegrated under the disputes between the Catholic and Protestant factions. In 1605 the Hapsburg archdukes, judging him to be politically incompetent, compelled him to entrust the conduct of Hungarian affairs to his brother, Matthias. In 1606 they recognized Matthias as their head and candidate for Rudolf's succession. Two years later Rudolf was forced to cede Hungary, Austria and Moravia to Matthias and to promise him the succession in Bohemia. When mutinous imperial troops under the archduke Leopold ravaged Bohemia with Leopold's support in 1611, the Bohemian Estates sought help from Matthias, whose army virtually held Rudolf prisoner in Prague until he abdicated Bohemia to Matthias in May. Matthias gained the imperial throne five months after Rudolf's death in January, 1612.

In *The Tempest*, Milan is clearly not a specific geographical place. The name may even be a barely disguised pun on 'my Land'. Milan is simply the centre of the terrain of existence, the capital of the dukedom, the territory for which Prospero is responsible. And Prospero can be anyone — you, me, he or she. I think that what we are dealing with here is the concept of the individual and his life — in the form of 'the ruler' and 'the ruler's dominions'. To be equal to the task of kingship, the ego as the centre of the personality must undergo a transformation. In hermetic texts this is often depicted as the old king being boiled naked in an alchemical vessel. Perhaps he must be dismembered or devoured. Sometimes, he must go down to the underworld, deep into the darkness of the realm of the dead (the collective unconscious). The reason for this, as Jung often pointed out, is that the transformation of the ego into the self always involves a deposing of the ego as the centre of the individual's personality and the creation of a centre much closer to the unconscious. This process, which Jung termed 'individuation', begins with a confrontation with the shadow.

> The shadow and the opposing will are the necessary condition for all actualization.
>
> (CW.11.p.196)

Because the shadow is that which is unconscious in the individual, it is usually obvious to everyone but the person himself. The more repressed it is, the more likely it is to be projected. The person will condemn and disparage those things in others which he is unconsciously dominated by in himself ("O, perfidious brother!"). The connection between spiritual and intellectual development and the shadowy demonic is a problem still with us. Jung wrote in 1946:

> But already we are fascinated by the possibilities of atomic fission and promise ourselves a Golden Age — the surest guarantee that the abomination of desolation will grow to limitless dimensions. And who or what is it that causes all this? It is none other than that harmless (!), ingenuous, inventive and sweetly reasonable human spirit who unfortunately is abysmally unconscious of the demonism that still clings to him. Worse, this spirit does everything to avoid looking himself in the face, and we all help him like mad.
>
> (CW.9.i.253)

The projected shadow then can be seen as a cloak, obscuring certain things from consciousness. Upon facing the shadow and looking through and beneath it, we find at first an undifferentiated psychic tangle of contents and functions, instincts and images — all in unconscious chaos, the *massa confusa* or *prima materia* of the Work, as the alchemists called it. That a person should voluntarily set out on this path to become conscious is rare. Usually, he is forced into it by some unsettling crisis in his life.

The shadow is a moral problem that challenges the whole ego personality, for no one can become conscious of the shadow without considerable moral effort. To become conscious of it involves recognizing the dark aspects of the personality as present and real. This act is the essential condition for any kind of self-knowledge, and it therefore, as a rule meets with considerable resistance.

(CW.9.pt.ii.p.8)

Prospero, the "prime duke" who was "so reputed/In dignity" and without a parallel in the liberal Arts, was surely a very refined and sophisticated gentleman. But certain elements are missing from that way of life. Since the time of the Greeks, man has always been considered as a unity of four elements: earth, water, fire and air. Symbolically, these can be seen as sensation, feeling, intuition and thinking. Jung called these the four functions of consciousness. Prospero, as he now describes himself to us and Miranda, is predominantly in the Air-Fire sector of Figure 2 below, which corresponds to intuitive thinking.

These four functional types correspond to the obvious means by which consciousness obtains its orientation to experience. *Sensation* (i.e. sense-perception) tells you that something exists; *thinking* tells you what it is; *feeling* tells you whether it is agreeable or not; and *intuition* tells you whence it comes and where it is going.[31]

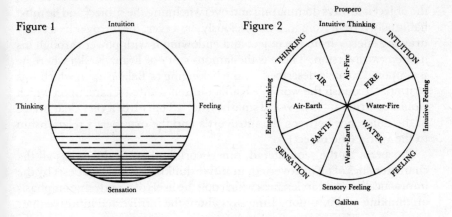

Figure 1. The Four Functions in pairs of polar opposites as Jung conceived of them. With Intuition shown as the superior function.

Figure 2. The Four Elements and the functions of Consciousness showing Prospero's and Caliban's superior function.

The way in which Jung conceived of these four functions was that the operation of one particular function normally excluded its polar opposite. Thinking represses feeling. Feeling excludes thinking. Thinking, however, can work in conjunction with intuition or sensation, the auxiliary functions. Usually, a person excels in one of the functions. This tends to become his 'superior' function. The opposing function is often neglected and left in an undeveloped, uncultivated state. This neglected function Jung termed the 'inferior' function.

The inferior function is infuriatingly slow. It is the source of many irritations and daily embarrassments. As it is extremely sensitive to criticism it always manages to cover-up and present the impression that all is well and it is functioning properly. In fact, most of its responses are either completely inappropriate or simply absent. It is only through the consistent attempt to assimilate the inferior function that it can gradually be raised to a higher level of consciousness. This is usually only accomplished by a corresponding lowering of the level of the superior function — a *sacrificium intellectus*, for example, in the case of thinking as the superior function.

Added to the ways that consciousness can function is the general attitude of the individual. Jung utilized the terms 'extraversion' and 'introversion' to describe a basic difference in attitude to the object. In the extravert conscious psychic energy constantly flows toward the object, but there is an unconscious return flow towards the subject. In the introvert it is as though the object is always dominating and overwhelming the subject and he must habitually retreat from it. Unconsciously, however, the introvert is secretly drawing energy from the object and endowing it with power through his hidden extraversion. There is the famous story of Franz Kafka where he is supposed to have described a cane belonging to Balzac upon which was written: "I smash the world". Kafka himself wanted a cane upon which would be written: "The world smashes me". That gives a very clear image of the difference between the introvert's and the extravert's relationship to the world (the object).

Prospero, as the sequestered, other-worldly, hermit-duke, has all the characteristics of an introverted, intuitive thinking type. He is beset by the impracticality and carelessness which dog the heels of an extreme emphasis on thinking and intuition. Jung says about the introverted intuitive that:

> Intensification of 'intuition' naturally often results in an extraordinary aloofness of the individual from tangible reality; he may even become a complete enigma to his own immediate circle.[32]

The introverted intuitive type is, in essence, the seer, the religious prophet, the shaman who is in contact with the slow and deep currents in the collective

9. *Alchemical library and laboratory,* from Tripus Aurea, Michael
Maier, 1677.

So many times must the heaven above the earth be reproduced, until the earth
becomes heavenly and spiritual, and heaven becomes earthly, and is joined to the
earth; then the work will be finished.

— *Philosophica Chemica, Theatr. Chem.,* I. 1602, p. 492

unconscious, and he communicates them to his tribe or society. He may
be an artist or a poet, but he is always inclined to the mystical. With all
his love of books, libraries and "secret studies", Prospero is obviously an
intellectual intuitive. But if the thinking and intuitive functions are well-
developed, we would expect that the opposing functions would suffer. Jung
describes the inferior function of the introverted intuitive in this way:

> The introverted intuitive's chief repression falls upon the sensation of
> the object. His unconscious is characterized by this fact. For we find
> in his unconscious a compensatory extraverted sensation of an archaic
> character. The unconscious personality may, therefore, best be described
> as an extraverted sensation-type of a rather low and primitive order.
> Impulsiveness and unrestraint are the characters of this sensation,
> combined with an extraordinary dependence upon the sense
> impression.[33]

We must also take note of the highly-developed thinking function's inferior
feeling. The invalidation and degradation of feeling in our culture is now
such a common phenomenon that most people take it for granted that feeling
evaluation is of minor importance in their lives, compared with the
judgements of thinking. James Hillman, a contemporary exponent of what
he has called 'archetypal psychology', is breaking new ground in the
understanding of the working of the feeling function. He writes: [34]

> So much is feeling the problem of the times that one could preposterously
> assert that the whole field of psychotherapy resulted from inadequacies
> of the feeling function. Our personal feeling problems are partly a
> collective result of the ages of repression, which have by no means been
> lifted by the confused enthusiasms of the eighteenth century nor by the
> pornographic delights of the mid-twentieth. Our feeling problems are
> collective problems, and we need new fantasies for them.

Presumably, in the Renaissance and during Elizabethan times the feeling
function was not under such heavy attack as it experienced in later centuries
— with Puritanism linking up with science and empiricism, leading into
imperialization and industrialization. But Shakespeare was far-seeing and
obviously aware of collective trends. It is noteworthy that the play which
has fascinated modern theatre more than any other in our time is
Shakespeare's *Hamlet*, in which "the native hue of resolution/ Is sickled
o'er with the pale cast of thought". We shall see from what follows that
Shakespeare was eminently aware of the necessity of feeling-values with
which to balance the one-sided emphasis on logos, the masculine intellect
and the spirit. In a much-needed contribution toward the phenomenology
of the feeling-function, Hillman says this about inferior feeling:

An early sign of inferior feeling is loss of contact with what one feels. The stuff and substance of the feeling function are usually feelings (not that the feeling function does not evaluate thoughts and sensations as well). But when the feeling function is inferior and goes underground as it were, with it goes an orienting awareness of how I feel, what I want, whom I like, etc., all of which is replaced by a general dryness in regard to myself and others, followed by indiscriminate complex-reactions: all sorts of displaced feelings, tears at the wrong time, wry jokes, peculiar attachments and enthusiasms, value-judgements creeping in where irrelevant or general undifferentiated mood swings of general elation or general depression.[35]

and:

. . . Inferior feeling, to sum it up, may be characterized by contamination with the repressed which tends to manifest, as the Scholastic would have said, in *ira* and *cupiditas*. Inferior feeling is loaded with anger and rage and ambition and aggression as well as greed and desire. Here we find ourselves with huge claims for love, with massive needs for recognition, and discover our feeling connection to life to be one vast expectation composed of thousands of tiny angry resentments. This expectation has been called an omnipotence fantasy, the expression of the abandoned child with his left-over feelings that nobody wants to take care of — but is this enough? Omnipotence is more than a content; rather, it expresses, as does the child, an impoverished functioning that insists upon more sway and exercise. Without this exercise, feeling turns upon itself, morbidly; we are envious, jealous, depressed, feeding on needs and their immediate gratification, then rushing out intermittently to meet someone to help or for help. The cat neglected becomes the unconscious tiger.[36]

Returning to Prospero, we can now anticipate a confrontation with the "unconscious tiger" of his unlived-out and repressed feeling side as well as the "unconscious primitive" of his inferior sensation.

The beauty of *The Tempest* is not that it is such a fantastic illustration of Jung's theories, but that, in it, we are shown how Nature herself is always attempting to right the balance of things out of balance. We are, as it were, standing for a miraculous moment beside the creator himself and allowed a glimpse into the most secret, inner workings of fate and destiny.

As the inferior function is the individual's weak spot, it is usually the door through which the Shadow comes into consciousness. The Shadow aims at consciousness and will not be kept out forever in the cold. One day it bursts through the door, and one can not keep it back anymore. Life is stronger than our wish for an unholy (not whole) peace. We must give in and allow defeat in order to achieve a new integration. With great precision and depth of insight, the poet shows us the beginnings of this process in the following lines:

Pros.   Now the condition.
　　　This King of Naples, being an enemy
　　　To me inveterate, hearkens my brother's suit;
　　　Which was, that he, in lieu o' th' premises
　　　Of homage and I know not how much tribute,
　　　Should presently extirpate me and mine
　　　Out of the dukedom, and confer fair Milan,
　　　With all the honours, on my brother: whereon,
　　　A treacherous army levied, one midnight
　　　Fated to th' purpose, did Antonio open
　　　The gates of Milan; and, i' th' dead of darkness,
　　　The ministers for th' purpose hurried thence
　　　Me and thy crying self.

Mir.   Alack, for pity!
　　　I not rememb'ring how I cried out then,
　　　Will cry it o'er again: it is a hint
　　　That wrings mine eyes to't.

Pros.   Hear a little further,
　　　And then I'll bring thee to the present business
　　　Which now's upon's; without the which, this story
　　　Were most impertinent.

Mir.   Wherefore did they not
　　　That hour destroy us?

Pros.   Well demanded, wench:
　　　My tale provokes that question. Dear, they durst not,
　　　So dear the love my people bore me; nor set
　　　A mark so bloody on the business; but
　　　With colours fairer painted their foul ends.
　　　In few, they hurried us abroad a bark,
　　　Bore us some leagues to sea; where they prepared
　　　A rotten carcase of a butt, not rigg'd,
　　　Nor tackle, sail, nor mast; the very rats
　　　Instinctively have quit it: there they hoist us,
　　　To cry to th' sea that roar'd to us; to sigh
　　　To the winds, whose pity, sighing back again,
　　　Did us but loving wrong.

Mir.   Alack, what trouble
　　　Was I then to you!

Pros.   O, a cherubin
Thou wast that did preserve me. Thou didst smile,
Infused with a fortitude from heaven,
When I have deck'd the sea with drops full salt,
Under my burthen groan'd; which rais'd in me
An undergoing stomach, to bear up —
Against what should ensure.

                                                     (I.ii.120-158)

In short, there has been a coup d'etat. Antonio, with the aid of the King
of Naples, decides to get rid of Prospero completely and to become "Absolute
Milan". In one fell swoop, Prospero is dethroned, banished from his
kingdom and finds himself with his baby daughter alone on the high seas
in a "rotten carcase of a butt" without "tackle, sail or mast". It is interesting
to note that what "preserves" Prospero throughout this terrifying ordeal
is *the child*. We can easily visualize it: Prospero, bracing himself in the
plunging hulk, shielding the bundle containing the infant from the drenching
waves, groaning, weeping tears that streamed down his face and "deck'd
the sea with drops full salt".

The link between tears and the sea is important. The immense, open
horizon of the sea is contained psychologically within the bright, fluid jewels
which spring from our eyes. The experiences of life can be ever so salty
and painful, but if we allow ('suffer') them, they can open our eyes to the
mysterious, unknowable spheres of life outside the constricted definitions
of our conscious egos. When we cry, we are no longer solitary, isolated egos.
The streams of our tears unite us to that unbounded ocean of grief and
poignant awareness which runs through the lives of humanity in all ages.
Who knows where tears really come from? They are as primeval as the sea
itself. Tears are a gift of the deeps. Without tears our lives are as parched
and barren as the rainless wastes of the Earth. When we cry, something
melts. Frozen life begins to flow again. Stagnant channels are at last
unblocked. Weeping unlocks the rusty doors of the heart and frees trapped
feeling-energy. It allows stifled joy to breathe again.

Propsero, crying his heart out in the huge unknown night of the sea, is
making that painful journey of the hero into the underworld. It is a journey
into the dark night of the soul, the night sea-journey, in which the hero
faces his own terrors and deepest doubts and uncertainties. Here, no
intellectual formulae 'hold water' and the false pride of the intellect is washed
away. If the hero survives, he emerges as a new man, with a fresh and
awakened understanding of the unconscious.

It is clear that this 'alchemical' knowledge was shared by a number of
Shakespeare's compatriots. To the Renaissance imagination — and this

was still very much alive in certain circles in Shakespeare's time —
melancholy was a Dark Lady of Mystery, as much at home in the night
as dreams and secretly able to inspire the artist with great genius — if he
dared woo her. For example, one of the key figures of Elizabethan music,
John Dowland, published a work in 1604 for the lute and viols, entitled:
Lachrimae, or Seaven Teares figured in Seaven Pavans. Each of the seven pavans
is given a title celebrating tears of a specific kind: 1) *Lachrimae Antiquae*, old
tears; 2) *Lachrimae Antiquae Novae*, old tears renewed; 3) *Lachrimae Gementes*,
sighing or groaning tears; 4) *Lachrimae Tristes*, sorrowful tears; 5) *Lachrimae
Coactae*, hardened or crystallized tears; 6) *Lachrimae Amantis*, lovers' tears;
and, finally, 7) *Lachrimae Verae*, true tears.

We have been taught to see tears as a sign of weakness, particularly in
men. But in Shakespeare's time this was not uniformly accepted. The art,
music and poetry of the Elizabethan Age and the early seventeenth century
was ornamented with these sparkling jewels of *melancholia* like dew-drops
on the petals of a black rose, diamonds on the robes of the Queen of the
Night. The occurrence of tears in Shakespeare's plays merits a whole study
of its own. Here, tears often seem to be condensations of tremendous clouds
of creative energy in turmoil. Often, the critical turning point in the hero
or heroine's progressive realization about the truth of their situation is
reflected in an image of tears. The tears which Othello and Lear weep directly
coincide with the opening of their previously closed minds to the truths which
they have unconsciously been repressing. As understanding dawns, they
weep, and, although both die soon after, a realization, a redemption has
taken place.

Othello: Then must you speak
          Of one that lov'd not wisely, but too well;
          Of one not easily jealous, but, being wrought,
          Perplexed in the extreme; of one whose hand,
          Like the base Indian, threw a pearl away
          Richer than all his tribe; of one whose subdu'd eyes,
          Albeit unused to the melting mood,
          Drops tears as fast as the Arabian trees
          Their medicinal gum.
                                                  (V.ii.345-354)

Lear: You do me wrong to take me out o' th' grave.
          Thou art a soul in bliss; but I am bound
          Upon a wheel of fire, that mine own tears
          Do scald like molten lead.
                                                  (IV.iv.45-48)

In *The Tempest* Shakespeare brings about the hero's realization of his error at a much earlier stage. But the whole question of error is on a much more subtle level than in the great tragedies of the previous years. Unless we examine the play carefully, we may miss the hero's error and see his banishment as merely the evil act of a scheming, treacherous brother. We then miss the fact that *Prospero has created this situation himself and from within himself*, mirroring the activity of Shakespeare's own psyche. Looking at the play as we would a myth or dream or fairy tale, we see that the characters are related in an internal way. Seeing through the superficial action of the play, we glimpse startling connections. However complete the different characterizations are in themselves, seeing them as reflections of differing aspects and functions of the same psyche gives the play a density of meaning far beyond any approach which looks at it simply as a 'flight into the world of make-believe' or as 'Shakespeare's farewell to the stage'.

What a different Prospero is shown to us now! How far away the court of Milan; how distant the cultured elegance, the centres of learning, the impressive libraries, the refined conversations, the wonders of art and civilization! All the props have been stripped away. Escape is no longer possible. He is naked and alone, at the mercy of the elemental powers. No, not quite alone, for there is a child with him. How strange, and yet, how apt, that a man who has lived in libraries, "rapt in secret studies" and "neglecting worldly ends" should now find himself the sole protector and provider for a little child in a situation of great physical peril. This child, however, is the seed of his salvation. Jung writes:

> The child is potential future. Hence the occurrence of the child motif in the psychology of the individual signifies as a rule an anticipation of future developments, even though at first sight it may seem like a retrospective configuration. Life is a flux, a flowing into the future, and not a stoppage or a backwash. It is therefore not surprising that so many of the mythological saviours are child gods. This agrees exactly with our experience of the psychology of the individual, which shows that the 'child' paves the way for a future change of personality. In the individuation process, it anticipates the figure that comes from the synthesis of conscious and unconscious elements in the personality. It is therefore a symbol which unites the opposites; a mediator, bringer of healing, that is, one who makes whole.

(CW.9.i.164)

Miranda's cherubin-smile was then the inspiration which kept Prospero from sinking into despair or worse — into the depths of the unconscious. It gave him "An undergoing stomach, to bear up/ Against what should ensure". Really caring for someone, especially a child, always restores balance in our lives. No matter how tiring or demanding that care may be, it is a meaningful activity and not a stupid, soulless labour of self-estranged egoistic existence. But powers beyond the ordinary have also been guiding Prospero. Shakespeare, with the voice of Prospero, calls them "divine", as we today might say they were "higher powers of the unconscious". The unconscious is not only 'below', it is 'above' as well! Whenever we suffer the death of a way of life, we always find ourselves 'at sea'. It is here that we discover the guiding powers which safely and surely bring us 'ashore' — to the extent that we entrust ourselves to life and sacrifice the meddling and worrying concern of the interfering ego-consciousness.

When we accept that whatever happens to us, however unjust or incomprehensible it may seem at the time, always carries a meaning, then we often become aware that we are not alone.

Mir.   How came we ashore?

Pros.   By Providence divine.
            Some food we had, and some fresh water, that
            A noble Neapolitan, Gonzalo,
            Out of his charity, who being then appointed
            Master of this design, did give us, with
            Rich garments, linens, stuffs and necessaries
            Which since have steaded much; so, of his gentleness,
            Knowing I lov'd my books, he furnished me
            From mine own library with volumes that
            I prize above my dukedom.

                                                      (I.ii.171-184)

How remarkable: that the "master of this design" should supply the exiles with food and water, clothes and choice books! Gonzalo, it is clear, is very fond of Prospero. This empathetic action of his — in contrast to his appointed and unpleasant role as the instrument of evil — strengthens our understanding of him as a personification of feeling. Gonzalo not only ensures that they have material necessaries but he stows aboard volumes which Prospero prizes above his dukedom.

Prospero now brings the story up to the present, and Miranda asks the question which has been "beating" in her mind:

Pros.   Here in this island we arriv'd; and here
            Have I, thy schoolmaster, made thee more profit
            Than other princess' can, that have more time
            For vainer hours, and tutors not so careful.

Mir.   Heavens thank you for 't! And now, I pray you, sir,
            For still 'tis beating in my mind, your reason
            For raising this sea-storm?

Pros.   Know thus far forth.
By accident most strange, bountiful Fortune,
(Now my dear lady) hath mine enemies
Brought to this shore; and by my prescience
I find my zenith doth depend upon
A most auspicious star, whose influence
If now I court not, but omit, my fortunes
Will ever after droop.

                                             (I.ii.171-184)

Instead of telling Miranda the answer to her question, Prospero side-steps the issue and says that "Fortune" has brought his enemies to these very same shores where he and she landed as castaways twelve years before. This is extraordinary in itself, but we are not given time to ponder it. His speech grows more excited. He adds, cryptically, that his "zenith" depends upon a "most auspicious star", whose influence he must not omit to "court", thereby introducing the first note of a theme which is to grow stronger as the action progresses: urgency. Then, as if sensing the approach of something Miranda is not yet ready to encounter, he takes up his mantle and abruptly puts the girl to sleep — with what seems to be a hypnotic induction.

Pros.   Here cease more questions:
Thou art inclin'd to sleep; 'tis a good dulness,
And give it way: I know thou canst not choose.
                                    (*Miranda sleeps*)
                                     (I.ii.184-187)

4. Ariel

10. Give fire to fire, Mercury to Mercury, & it is enough for you.

"The golden age of alchemy was the sixteenth and the first half of the
seventeenth century. At that time a storm bird did indeed escape from a
spiritual vessel which the daemons must have felt was a prison. As I have
said, the alchemists were all for not letting Mercurius escape. They wanted
to keep him in the bottle in order to transform him: for they believed, like
Petasios, that lead (another arcane substance) was 'so bedevilled and shameless
that all who wish to investigate it fall into madness through ignorance'.
The same was said of the elusive Mercurius who evades every grasp — a real
trickster who drove the alchemists to despair."
— C.G. Jung (CW.13.p.203)

In the next few lines of the play Shakespeare releases a powerful daimon
onto the stage:

> *Pros.*   Come away, servant, come. I am ready now.
>   Approach, my Ariel, come.
>
>   *Enter* Ariel
>
> *Ari.*   All hail, great master! grave sir, hail! I come
>   To answer thy best pleasure; be 't to fly,
>   To swim, to dive into the fire, to ride
>   On the curl'd clouds, to thy strong bidding task
>   Ariel and all his quality.

                                              (I.ii.187-193)

This is not the Prospero of whom we have been hearing, not the washed-up castaway who lost his dukedom through absent-minded negligence. This is no hazy, visionary drop-out, but a master shaman with immense authority and power to command the very elements. It is of *this* Prospero that Frances Yates must be thinking when she writes that Shakespeare "shows us an infinitely wise and beneficent figure, working for moral goodness and reform, a marvellous evocation of the Renaissance magus in his full imaginative and creative power".[37]

No one would argue with Frances Yates over this beautiful description of Prospero as we see him on the island, twelve years after his exile. But the really interesting thing is *how* did he achieve this incredible stature? She offers no explanation. And she is not alone. Sifting through the mass of Shakespearean scholarship on *The Tempest*, one is struck by the remarkable lacuna which Prospero's transformation seems to create in any discussion of the play. G. Wilson Knight describes pre-exile Prospero as "Plato's philosopher-king betrayed by a Machiavellian 'policy' "[38] and the later Prospero as "a matured and fully self-conscious embodiment of those moments of fifth act transcendental speculation to which earlier tragic heroes, including Macbeth, were unwillingly forced".[39] We are not told how he becomes this "fully self-conscious embodiment" — only that "he has established himself on his island where, in loneliness he, with Miranda by his side, has slowly perfected his art."

Why this blindspot? Why is it that no one asks the obvious question: How does the Prospero of the pre-exile years in Milan (P_1) become the "infinitely wise and beneficent" Prospero of the post-exile years on the island (P_2)? It is not just a matter of course that, given twelve years on a desert island, P_1 becomes P_2. There is a definite and specific transform of $P_1 \rightarrow$ (into) P_2. Prospero undergoes a real and total change in that time.

Because of the electrifying brilliance and charismatic vitality of the figure of Ariel, we tend to overlook the fact that he is Prospero's *servant*. In other words, what we are dealing with is Prospero's *own* extended authority over the elements of his own nature. My feeling about this is that Ariel is none other than the Mercurius hailed by the alchemists as *both* the *prima materia* of the Work and the highest transformation of it into the *lapis* as the highest goal *as well as* the process which lies between and the means by which it is effected. He is the beginning, the middle and the end of the Work. He is therefore the mediator, the healer of imperfections and the Universal Medicine itself. He is an aspect of (Prospero's) psyche personified. Shakespeare, like the alchemists, could personify him because he is a universal possibility, inherent within Everyman, an archetypal image of what Jung called "the transcendent function". This mysterious principle in Jung's psychology is the "fifth function" (see earlier description of the functions on page   ) of which Jung wrote:

> The secret of alchemy was in fact the transcendent function, the transformation of personality through the blending and fusion of the noble with the base components, of the differentiated with the inferior functions, of the conscious with the unconscious.
>
> (CW.9.ii.p.220)

For the time being then, let us say that Mercurius/Ariel is the living symbol of the ever-present, inherent possibility of psychic self-transformation. Now, let us return to the play and watch Ariel in action.

Pros.   Hast thous, spirit,
            Performed to point the tempest that I bade thee?

Ari.   To every article.
            I boarded the king's ship; now on the beak,
            Now in the waist, the deck, in every cabin,
            I flam'd amazement: sometime I'd divide,
            And burn in many places; on the topmast,
            The yards and boresprit, would I flame distinctly,
            Then meet and join. Jove's lightnings, the precursors
            O' th' dreadful thunder-claps, more momentary
            And sight-outrunning were not: the fire and cracks
            Of sulphurous roaring the most mighty Neptune
            Seem to besiege, and make his bold waves tremble,
            Yea, his dread trident shake.

Pros.   My brave spirit!
            Who was so firm, so constant, that this coil
            Would not infect his reason?

Ari.   Not a soul
            But felt a fever of the mad, and play'd
            Some tricks of desperation. All but mariners
            Plung'd in the foaming brine, and quite the vessel;[40]
            Then all afire with me the King's son, Ferdinand,
            With hair up-staring, — then like reeds, not hair, —
            Was the first man that leap'd; cried, "Hell is empty,
            And all the devils are here."

                                        (I.ii.193-214)

St. Elmo's fire was, of course, sometimes called St. Hermes' fire by the Italians, and we know from a number of alchemical sources that the character of the classical Hermes was accurately repeated later in the figure of Mercurius. As Jung pointed out, many alchemical treatises define Mercurius simply as fire. In his superb Eranos lectures on ''The Spirit Mercurius'' which he gave in 1942, Jung said:

> The *aqua mercurialis* is even a divine fire. This fire is 'highly vaporous' (*vaporosus*). Indeed, Mercurius is really the only fire in the whole procedure . . . He is, in fact, as another text says, 'the universal and scintillating fire of the light of nature, which carries the heavenly spirit within it'.
>
> . . . Mercurius, the revelatory light of nature, is also hell-fire, which in some miraculous way is none other than a rearrangement of the heavenly, spiritual powers in the lower, chthonic world of matter, thought already in St. Paul's time to be ruled by the devil. Hell-fire, the true energetic principle of evil, appears here as the manifest counterpart of the spiritual and the good, and as essentially identical with it in substance. After that, it can surely cause no offence when another treatise says that the mercurial fire is the 'fire in which God himself burns in divine love'. We are not deceiving ourselves if we feel in scattered remarks of this kind the breath of true mysticism.
>
> (CW.13.p.209-10)

We say ''Amen'' to this — as well as to Shakespeare's unmatched poetic genius as it dances through the images of Ariel's speech where he recounts his scintillating epiphany on board the king's ship: crackling up and down the masts like lightning, suddenly flaming amazement in the cabins, dividing and burning in different places all over the ship, playing over the bodies and clothes of the men, and, in general, inspiring such panic that the men leap into the sea. Ariel-as-Mercurius is thus playing the part of the transcendent function in effecting, or mediating, a rapprochement between the conscious and the unconscious functions. We have already seen how the men on board the boat, coming from Milan and the mainland, are representatives of consciousness. Now, 'Fortune' has brought them close enough to the island (a split-off part of consciousness), to come within the field of the forces working toward integration. But before they can all meet, the representatives of the conscious, superior functions have to lose their sense of assumed 'superiority', and they must be immersed in the sea of the unconscious and be baptised — and touched by the fire of the transcendent function. Ariel is thus, in one way, an externalization of Prospero's desire for reconciliation among the various cut-off parts of himself, previously rejected and projected onto the most suitable objects in his world. The fact that the dunking in the sea which the men experience is no ordinary dunking is clear from Ariel's reply to Prospero's concerned question about their safety:

Ari.   Not a hair perish'd;
On their sustaining garments not a blemish,
But fresher than before —

                                                    (I.ii.217-219)

Shakespeare leaves no room for doubt as to the importance of this immersion in the ocean. As Jung said: ". . . the way into any higher development leads through water"[41] The passengers from the mainland must, like Prospero himself, be brought into a relationship with the unconscious.

Emphasizing the symbolic nature of this baptism, the poet has Ariel say that their clothes are "fresher than before". What miraculous substance is this water into which they have leapt? This water which doesn't behave like water, this 'dry water'? I feel that we have here another hint of the alchemical composition of *The Tempest*. Quoting from Jung's work on Mercurius again, we have the chance of further freeing the spirit of this tricky character from the petrifying spell of literalism. For we must not think that we can ever catch him alive in our nets of words. It is of his essence that he can not be pinned down:

> Mercurius was first understood pretty well everywhere as *hydra argyrum* (Hg), quicksilver or argentum vivum (Fr. vif argent or argent vive). As such, it was called *vulgaris* (common) or *crudus*. As a rule, *mercury philosophicus* was specifically distinguished from this, as an avowedly arcane substance that was conceived to be present in *mercurius crudus*, and then, again, to differ from it completely. It was the true object of the alchemical procedure. Quicksilver, because of its fluidity and volatility, was defined as water. A popular saying is: "Aqua manus non malefaciens" (the water that does not make the hands wet).
>
>   (CW.13.p.207)

The nature of Mercurius is that he is not bound to any one form. Indeed, one of his epithets is *shape-shifter*. Our logical, linear minds would like to grasp him as fire or as water and not allow him to change. But it is this very literalness which bogs us down. By refusing him free-rein to manifest the unknown, we repress his saving grace and, instead of moving light-footed through the troubles that beset us, we drag our feet in dull-witted despondency. We have thus exchanged Hermes' winged sandals for a pair of clumsy, leaden boots.

Hermes/Mercurius is indeed a tricky character. His nimbleness, agility, swiftness and clever deftness make him the archetype of subtlety. Yet, although there are definite aspects of deception and roguery associated with him, he is known as "the friendliest of gods to men"[42] This quality of elusiveness is vividly conjured by Jung:

> It was certainly quicksilver, but a very special quicksilver, 'our'
> Mercurius, the essence, moisture, or principle behind or within the
> quicksilver — that indefinable, fascinating, irritating, elusive thing which
> attracts an unconscious projection. The 'philosophic' Mercurius, this
> *servus fugitivus* or *cervus fugitivus* (fugitive slave or stag) . . .
>   (CW.13.p.211)

Hermes, the "Lord of the Roads", is the patron of travellers as well as thieves and highwaymen. If he is the "god who guides", he is also the "god who leads astray".[43] We know from the Homeric *Hymn to Hermes* that he was the only appointed messenger to Hades. As Hermes Chthonius, he was the *psychopomp* who led soul *down into* the underworld as well as *back up out* of it. Today, we do not speak of Hades or the Underworld, but rather of the unconscious.[44] Hermes has thus been recognized as the ideal patron for psychotherapy.[45] As "god of borders" and all borderline areas and states, Hermes is the perfect protector for any process involving the integration of conscious and unconscious elements.

In *The Tempest* Ariel is the agent of this work. In the creation of the figure of Ariel, Shakespeare's poetic genius is *personifying* the alchemists' treasured principle of transmutation, Mercurius: that psychic quicksilver which Jung called "the transcendent function".

The alchemists gave extraordinarily graphic descriptions of Mercurius, but nowhere do they succeed as Shakespeare in personifying him as a psychic presence to the degree that we meet him in the person of "Ariel and all his quality". The following is one such description from a classical alchemical work, the *Aurelia Occulta* (1659)[46]:

> I am the egg of nature, known only to the wise, who in piety and modesty
> bring forth from me the microcosm, which was prepared for mankind
> by Almighty God, but given only to the few, while the many long for
> it in vain, that they may do good to the poor with my treasure and not
> fasten their souls to perishable gold. By the philosophers I am named
> Mercurius; my spouse is the (philosophic) gold; I am the old dragon,
> found everywhere on the globe of the earth, father and mother, young
> and old, very strong and very weak, death and resurrection, visible and
> invisible, hard and soft; I descend into the earth and ascend to the
> heavens, I am the highest and the lowest, the lightest and the heaviest;
> often the order of nature is reversed in me; I contain the light of nature;
> I am dark and light; I came forth from heaven and earth; I am known
> and yet do not exist at all; by virtue of the sun's rays all colours shine
> in me, and all metals. I am the carbuncle of the sun, the most noble
> purified earth, through which you may change copper, iron, tin, and
> lead into gold.

To put it succinctly: Ariel is no private familiar of Prospero, nor is he a peculiar invention of Shakespeare's. He is no foreign creature from outer space. He is rather the embodiment of the imagination, the "Divine Body of Man". *The exercise of the transcendent function is the creative play of the imagination.*

To return to the play, then: Ariel has succeeded in bringing the relevant members of the ship's company to the island. He tells Prospero that he has "dispers'd them 'bout the isle" as Prospero bade him. But:

> Ari.   The King's son have I landed by himself;
> Whom I left cooling of the air with sighs.
> In an odd angle of the isle, and sitting,
> His arms in this sad knot.
>
> (I.ii.220-224)

By singling out Ferdinand, Ariel thus indirectly informs us that the prince is a key figure among the newcomers to the island. Ferdinand is the son of Alonso, King of Naples. We remember that he was the first to jump from the 'spooked' ship. He is described as being "at prayers" with his father, during the storm. Coming thus from the mainland, he is a part of the 'mainland consciousness', the masculine emphasis on logos, but he is of a new generation of spirit, one which is younger and more open to soul, the inner deepening and reflection symbolized by 'prayer'.

Not all of the ship's company have been drawn into Prospero's 'magnetic field', however. We learn that Ariel has "stow'd" the crew "all under hatches" and left them asleep in the ship — which he has safely hidden in a "deep nook" of the island. The rest of the fleet are "Bound sadly home for Naples;/ Supposing that they saw the King's ship wrack'd,/ And his great person perish". (I.ii.235-7)

Next follows a dialogue between Prospero and Ariel about the time of day and the urgency of the action.

> Pros.   Ariel, thy charge
> Exactly is perform'd: but there's more work.
> What is the time o' th' day?
>
> Ari.   Past mid season.
>
> Pros.   At least two glasses. The time 'twixt six and now
> Must by us both be spent most preciously.

This is an odd exchange, and Kermode, in his footnotes to the Arden edition of *The Tempest*, remarks that such precision "would be very curious in Elizabethan drama."

Shakespeare, in fact, refers to the time element *no less than five more times*

during the course of the play. He is at great pains to inform us that the
entire action from this point on occurs within *three to four hours*. Why?
No commentator has yet offered any coherent explanation. It has been lamely
suggested that Shakespeare is trying to conform to the strict prerequisites
of time in classical drama. Of course, this constant harping on the shortness
of the time does give a dramatic urgency to the play, but is this the whole
reason?

I would like to suggest that these lines refer to an astrological configuration
or aspect of precisely three to four hours' duration. Prospero has already
told us that he has discovered through his "prescience" (a predictive ability
every good intuitive astrologer would possess) that his zenith depends
upon —

> A most auspicious star, whose influence
> If now I court not, but omit, my fortunes
> Will ever after droop.

(I.ii.180-184)

What more could we ask of our greatest bard than that he would crown
his life's work with a mythologem which transcends all his previous insights?
In earlier plays Shakespeare often alludes to vital correspondences between
men's fate and the stars. But nowhere do we have a hero who is so consciously
striving towards an understanding of the synchronicity between macrocosm
and microcosm. In the final scenes of all the last four plays this awareness
is articulated, but it is only in *The Tempest* that we have it present from the
beginning. In *Cymbeline* (V.v.464-5) the Soothsayer says:

> The fingers of the powers above do tune
> The harmony of this peace.

I will leave it to the astrologers to work out the tantalizing problem of
which particular star (planet) and aspect Prospero is referring to in this
speech.*

The idea of courting the influence of the planets, however, is one that
would have been common knowledge to anyone aware of the magical
traditions of the sixteenth and early seventeenth centuries. I have earlier
referred to Agrippa's philosophy of magic in the discussion of John Dee.
Behind Agrippa, however, is the imposing figure of Marsilio Ficino
(1433-1499), the Florentine mystic who, under the patronage of Cosimo
de' Medici, translated the *Corpus Hermeticum* into Latin, as well as many
key texts of Plato and the Neo-Platonists. Ficino's greatest work, however,

*See note [21] to Part III.

was in attempting to counterbalance the Church's petrification into a sterile system of monotheism which repressed every manifestation of the ancient traditions of polytheism, i.e., the pagan gods. His defence of astrological magic, a very dangerous enterprise in those times, was to keep the door open into the rich areas of polytheistic thought for some time to come. Agrippa, writing in the early sixteenth century, hermetically thieved a great deal from Ficino, and his work considerably influenced Giordano Bruno; and with Bruno we are in the England of Elizabeth, Sidney, Marlowe, Raleigh, John Dee and Shakespeare.

This is what Ficino wrote about courting influences of the 'stars':[47]

> Our spirit is consonant with the heavenly rays which, occult or manifest, penetrate everything. We can make it still more consonant, if we vehemently direct our affections towards the star from which we wish to receive a certain benefit . . . above all, if we apply the song and light suitable to the astral deity and also the odour, as in the hymns of Orpheus addressed to the cosmic deities.

Ficino, and Diacetto after him, worked out numerous ways to 'draw' the influences of a particular planet — through specific imagery in song, musical modes and the use of scents and colours. Notice that Ficino speaks of "the astral deity", making no distinction between the planet and a god. In our century, through the work of C. G. Jung, we have come to recognize these forces as archetypal powers in the collective unconscious. To 'court the influence' of such powers is thus to become conscious of such unconscious deities in our life. Just how Prospero is doing this is not revealed, but we are meant to be aware that he is doing it. In fact, at this point in the play, the audience has no idea what Prospero is really up to.

In the next section of the play Shakespeare takes us with him right inside the heart of the 'alchemical laboratory' where we are allowed a glimpse of the Work itself. It starts with an intimate quarrel between Prospero and Ariel. Ariel wishes to have his liberty. Prospero says that his time is not yet "out". Ariel replies that he has done "worthy service", told no lies, has not deceived Prospero and has not grumbled. He reminds Prospero of his promise to let him off. Prospero is adamant:

Pros.   Dost thou forget
From what a torment I did free thee?

Ari.   No.

Pros.   Thou dost, and think'st it much to tread the ooze
Of the salt deep,
To run upon the sharp wind of the north,

> To do me business in the veins o' th' earth
> When it is bak'd with frost.

Ari.   I do not sir.

Pros.   Thou liest, malignant thing!

(I.ii.250-257)

Several interesting things emerge from this exchange. We are again reminded that Ariel is at home in all the elements, emphasizing his integrating and connection-making activity. We are also made aware of his more shifty, evasive and unstable side. Prospero must contain him with rigorous watchfulness, just as an alchemist would have to treat a cloud of volatized mercury to prevent it escaping. Sublimation on a psychic level is just as tricky a process as it is in the laboratory, among retorts, alembics and ovens. Lastly, we learn that Ariel was once upon a time freed by Prospero. This is a fascinating revelation, and now we hear more about it:

Pros.   Has thou forgot
> The foul witch Sycorax, who with age and envy
> Was grown into a hoop? has thou forgot her?

Ari.   No, sir.

Pros.   Thou hast. Where was she born? speak; tell me.

Ari.   Sir, in Argier.

Pros.   O, was she, so? I must
> Once in a month recount what thou hast been,
> Which thou forget'st. This damn'd witch Sycorax,
> For mischiefs manifold, and sorceries terrible
> To enter human hearing, from Argier,
> Thou know'st, was banish'd: for one thing she did
> They would not take her life. Is not this true?

Ari.   Ay, sir.

Pros.   This blue-eyed hag was hither brought with child,
> And here was left by th' sailors. Thou, my slave,
> As thou report'st thyself, was then her servant;
> And, for thou wast a spirit too delicate
> To act her earthy and abhorr'd commands
> Refusing her grand hests, she did confine thee,
> By help of her most potent ministers,
> And in her most unmitigable rage,
> Into a cloven pine; within which rift
> Imprisoned thou didst painfully remain

A dozen years; within which space she died,
And left thee there; where thou didst vent thy groans
As fast as mill-wheels strike. Then was this island
Save for the son that she did litter here,
A freckled whelp hag-born — not honoured with
A human shape.

Ari.   Yes, Caliban her son.

Pros.   Dull thing, I say so; he, that Caliban,
Whom now I keep in service. Thou best know'st
What torment I did find thee in; thy groans
Did make wolves howl, and penetrate the breasts
Of ever-angry bears; it was a torment
To lay upon the damn'd, which Sycorax
Could not again undo. it was mine Art
When I arriv'd and heard thee, that made gape
The pine, and let thee out.

Ari.   I thank thee, master.

Pros.   If thou more murmur'st, I will rend an oak,
And peg thee in his knotty entrails, till
Thou hast howl'd away twelve winters.

Ari.   Pardon, master:
I will be correspondent to command,
And do my spiriting gently.

Pros.   Do so; and after two days
I will discharge thee.

Ari.   That's my noble master!
What shall I do? say what, what shall I do?

                                        (I.ii.257-300)

Here, with the person of Sycorax, the "foul witch", we have reached
the alchemical heart of the matter, the *prima materia*. In another of the play's
extraordinary images we are told that this foul creature "was grown into
a hoop" with "age and envy". Thus, in one exact image Shakespeare has
indicated where the source of wholeness lies: in the witch herself, bent into
a hoop, synonymous with the circle, everywhere symbolic of completeness.
At the same time he has indicated the source of Evil, the obstacle to wholeness:
the crippled life-energy which has been maimed by the destructive power
of a malicious feminine envy. The figure of the witch then calls for a very
careful study if we are to touch the deeper levels of meaning in the play.

5. Sycorax

11. **His nurse is the earth.**

Sycorax: the very sounds of the hissing, cutting syllables give us an immediate intimation of a being to be dreaded. Her name is filled with a poisonous blue-black rage. Do we need to know any further that her name means "Sow-raven" (Gk. sy = sow; corax = raven)? She is definitely a power to be reckoned with.

Commentators on Shakespeare have always noted the resemblance between Sycorax and the classical figures of the witch of antiquity. Colin Still in his book on *The Tempest* says:[48]

> . . . the text of the Play ascribes to Sycorax all the distinctive attributes with which the mythical Evil Woman is endowed.
>
> We have seen that among the many versions of this Evil Woman of tradition are the Zoharic Lilith, the Strange Woman of Proverbs, the Great Whore of Revelation, the Egyptian Nepthys, the Hebrew Tehom and the Chaldean Omoroca or Thalath, whose Greek equivalent is Hecate.

Kermode says:[49]

> Caliban's mother, though associated with reports of devil-worship and witchcraft in the New World, belongs to the Old. She is a powerful witch, deliberately endowed with many of the qualities of classical witches,

but also possessing a clearly defined place in the contemporary demonological scheme. She is a practitioner of 'natural' magic, a goetist who exploited the universal sympathies, but whose power is limited by the fact that she could command, as a rule, only devils and the lowest orders of spirits. Prospero, on the other hand, is a theurgist, whose Art is to achieve supremacy over the natural world by holy magic.

Robert Graves sees her as a particularly virulent form of *The White Goddess:* [50]

I remarked that poets can well be judged by the accuracy of their portrayal of the White Goddess. Shakespeare knew and feared her . . . He shows her with great sincerity in *Macbeth* as the Triple Hecate presiding over the witches' cauldron, for it is her spirit that takes possession of Lady Macbeth and inspires her to murder King Duncan; and as the magnificent and wanton Cleopatra by love of whom Anthony is destroyed. Her last appearance in the plays is as the 'damn'd witch' Sycorax in *The Tempest*. Shakespeare in the person of Prospero claims to have dominated her by his magic books, broken her power and enslaved her monstrous son Caliban — though not before extracting his secrets from him under colour of kindness.

Graves does not tell us what these "secrets" are, which Prospero has "extracted" from Caliban. He, like most commentators, sees Sycorax simply as a contrast to Prospero — her black magic emphasizing his white.

We have Jung to thank for pointing out that the witch stands for *mater natura* or the original matriarchal state of the unconscious, which becomes negative because of the attitude of the conscious ego. Marie-Louise von Franz has deepened and expanded Jung's work on the mother-complex considerably. In her book *Shadow and Evil in Fairy Tales* she states that —

. . . evil does not come from the principle of consciousness, but from a neglected archetype of the unconscious, from the witch.

The witch is an archetypal figure of the Great Mother. She is the neglected mother Goddess, the Goddess of the earth, the mother Goddess in her destructive aspect. [51]

I have not yet discussed archetypes in relation to *The Tempest*, but I have already introduced Ariel as the personification of a certain archetypal perspective, called by the alchemists "Mercurius" — and by the Greeks "Hermes". According to Jung, an archetype can be apprehended in two ways, as instinct or as image. An archetypal image is thus a way of personifying a collective (instinctual) energy. It does not ever fully express it.

It is important not to lose sight of the fact that we are trying to understand *The Tempest psychologically* rather than dramatically or linguistically. Prospero, as the Duke of Milan, as we have seen, identified over-much with the conscious attitudes of the (masculine) intellect. Jung's words to Count Keyserling would have applied equally to Prospero in Milan:[52]

> The negative relationship to the mother is always an affront to nature, unnatural. Hence, distance from the earth, identification with the father, heaven, light, wind, spirit, Logos. Rejection of the earth, of what is below, dark, feminine. Negative relationship to material things, also to children. Flight from personal feelings.

Prospero's deposition and subsequent banishment from Milan can be seen symbolically as the overthrow of an attitude of tyranny-on-the-part-of-the-conscious toward the forces of the collective unconscious. In the process of this breakdown, the persona (the social mask) disintegrates. Unconscious influences predominate. Prospero must confront the living psychic forces which have broken through into consciousness. First of all, he must come to terms with the shadow. Behind that again, there is the anima, the feminine within himself, the soul, which he has largely rejected. In the beginning this was covered by a mass of confused, negative feeling. There was little clarity or differentiation among the unconscious contents. As Marie-Louise von Franz says:[53]

> ... seen from the angle of the unconscious, when an archetype becomes conscious, it is a process of incarnation. The archetypal image loses some of its plenitude, becoming more specific. This entails a narrowing in. I represented the archetypes as contents, or nuclei, in the unconscious. But they are more likely in a kind of soup in which everything is contaminated by everything else. Thus an archetype which is in the unconscious is identical with the whole unconsciousness. It is its own contrast; it is everything; masculine and feminine, dark and light, and its own opposite. Everything overlaps; only when an archetype approaches the threshold of consciousness does it become more distinct.

How appropriate that Shakespeare should present us with the figure of Sycorax — that ugly image of the neglected feminine which has turned fierce and vengeful. Sycorax, unseen and invisible, brings a dark power and a depth to the play which, before, had been lacking.

Much has been written on the possible sources for Sycorax and many attempts have been made to figure out exactly who she is. With Shakespeare's obvious vagueness about her past, there is fertile ground for speculation. But, really, it is not necessary to know her address and passport number. She is that archetypal perspective which, crippled, cripples. She personifies the angry Great Mother, the feminine in its wrathful, destructive and paralyzing aspect.

When Prospero asks Ariel where the witch was born, and Ariel answers, "Sir, in Argier", Prospero sardonically replies, "O, was she so?" reminding Ariel that Sycorax, like himself, was banished ("for sorceries terrible to enter human hearing") and came, *like Prospero*, with child, to the island. Prospero thus avoids answering where she was born, because she was born in the depths of the unconscious. Instead, he stresses her connection to the island. It is clear that we have entered upon a discussion of psychic events and experiences. It is a mistake to take all this literally.

The same holds true for the endless arguments as to the specific locality of the island. Again, Shakespeare is deliberately vague, referring to the Mediterranean as well as to the Bermudas. Geography, however, is not the main issue. The island is first and foremost an image of something cut-off, something isolated (L. *insula*) and insulated. It is only *after* his deposition that Prospero comes to a conscious relationship with the forces of the unconscious — represented initially by Sycorax. Pre-exile Prospero in Milan (P_1) is completely estranged from this side of his existence. Diagrammatically, it would appear like this:

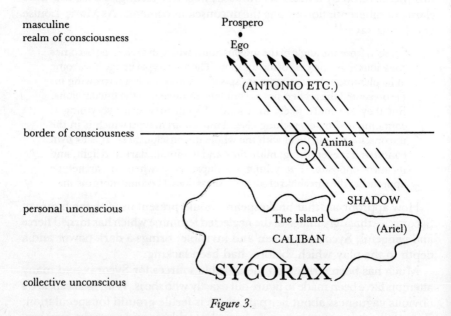

Figure 3.

At this stage we have no clear differentiation of the mother-complex (Sycorax) from the rest of the unconscious. Ariel is also there, trapped in his tree on the island — as well as Caliban, still unborn, within the mother-complex.

When Prospero loses his dukedom, life breaks in with a sudden violence. In his banishment into the tremendous sea of the unconscious, he begins to become aware of that of which he was previously unconscious. This is a critical point where many have drowned (i.e., been submerged in the unconscious) or have become inflated (due to the emergence of the unconscious contents). As Jung often said, consciousness *is* differentiation. And so, we would expect a development towards differentiation when Prospero reaches the island. And this is what happens. The island, by the way, is never really *his* — though through the confrontation with its forces, he gradually grows familiar with it and is able to connect its life with that on the mainland.

It is my hunch that Prospero, following the ruling, patriarchal tradition of Western culture, rejected the feminine in order to escape its claims of emotional involvement and feeling commitment. But you cannot do this and expect no repercussions. As Marie-Louise von Franz says: [54]

> If you hurt a living principle in the form of the actual woman, or deeper even, of the feminine principle per se, you do not recognize it in its life value, even if it is contrary to the philosophical outlook, and then it turns negative.

When something in the unconscious is rejected, it usually turns around and lames something else. In this case, it is the transcendent function which gets it. There are many examples of this kind of bewitching paralysis in myth and fairy-tale. In commenting on one such fairy story, von Franz describes this exactly: [55]

> And in the story . . . you see that it is the archetype of the Great Mother who avenges herself by attacking the transcendent function, the process of becoming conscious, the process towards individuation; and that is worse than if she attacked the conscious part directly.

There is no better image in our literature for the agony of the imprisoned transcendent function — trapped in the dead wood of the negative mother complex — than Ariel shut up within the "cloven pine". Prospero remembers this vividly:

> *Pros.*   Thou best know'st
> What torment I did find thee in; thy groans
> Did make wolves howl, and penetrate the breasts
> Of ever-angry bears: it was a torment
> To lay upon the damn'd.
>
>   (I.ii.286-90)

The fact that Ariel's cries were felt by wild beasts is an indication of how deep the complex reached. It struck at the very roots of being, the deepest core of the instinctual self and that is why the animals responded. I am sure that there is an echo in all this of Prospero's experience of the hell of his own isolation and estrangement from life.

Ariel was trapped within the tree twelve years. This is the same length of time Prospero must spend on the island. The number is mentioned a third time when we hear Prospero threatening to ''peg'' Ariel within the ''knotty entrails'' of an oak until he has ''howl'd away twelve winters''. Prospero is playing for high stakes and he needs Ariel's total co-operation. There is the feeling in his excitement that something very significant is now reaching a culmination. As being equal to three times the sacred number of four (symbolizing wholeness), the number twelve is a numinous and powerful figure. Jung says:

> The number 12 is presumably a time symbol, with subsidiary meaning of the twelve labours (of Heracles) that have to be performed for the unconscious before one can get free.
>
> (CW9,i,p.241)

Although we hear very little about it, we can be certain that Prospero's life on the island these past twelve years has not been a bed of roses. Ariel's groans are an externalized image for Prospero's own pain. That this suffering was not meaningless is evident in Prospero's greater maturity and power. His greater insight has not fallen out of the skies; it has been won through acceptance of his fate: he has suffered (allowed) his suffering. Jung, in a letter to a pupil, hinted at the intensity of the confrontation with the unconscious:[56]

> Do you know Keyserling's dreams? And do you think he could safely stand the shock of glimpsing the face of his own shadow? I have yet to meet a man who has done so without shuddering, and who did not talk a little deliriously afterwards. You can hear echoes of it in Meyrink's gruesome fantasies. And it is characteristic that (at least in his books) he has still not got over it.

A decade or so later, Jung had had more experience. In the paper ''Archetypes of the Collective Unconscious'' (1934-54), he wrote:

> True, whoever looks into the mirror of the water will see first of all his face. Whoever goes to himself risks a confrontation with himself. The mirror does not flatter, it faithfully shows whatever looks into it; namely, the face we never show to the world because we cover it with the persona, the mask of the actor. But the mirror lies behind the mask and shows the true face.

This confrontation is the first test of courage on the inner way, a test sufficient to frighten off most people, for the meeting with oneself belongs to the more unpleasant things that can be avoided so long as we can project everything negative into the environment. But if we are able to see our own shadow and can bear knowing about it, then a small part of the problem has already been solved: we have at least brought up the personal unconscious.

(CW9,pt.1,p20)

Prospero's first task on the island was to come to grips with the negativity he had been projecting onto his environment. Once he had begun to do this he could go through that door which is the shadow into the boundless realms of the collective unconscious. Goethe, very aptly, calls this area of the psyche, "The Mothers" — because it is the primeval matrix of consciousness: [57]

Mephis.	Even to speak of them dismays the bold.
	These are The Mothers.

Faust: Mothers?

Mephis.   Stand you daunted?

Faust: The Mothers! Mothers — sound with wonder haunted.

Mephis.   True, goddess unknown to mortal mind,
And named indeed with dread among our kind.
To reach them, delve below earth's deepest floors;
And that we need them, all the blame is yours.

We have not answered the question as to how Prospero "made gape/ The pine" and let Ariel out. He says it was "mine Art". What does he mean? It is customary to see this as referring to some fantastic, supernatural power which Prospero wields through his secret knowledge of magic. True, Prospero is identified with the Renaissance magus. He wears a mantle, carries a staff and has esoteric books. He practises astrology, controls the elements, apparently raises a storm at sea and has at least one spirit under his command. As C. J. Sisson puts it, "The effectiveness of *The Tempest* as a play requires that some measure of assent should be given by the audience to this portrait of a magician". [58] This is true, but, nevertheless, I do not feel that Prospero means magic when he says "Art". It is more likely that he means alchemy, which was known as the 'Black Art'.

My interpretation of the play stands or falls on this point — and the reader may find that my way of understanding is not the only one possible. That's good. I do not want to have the last word. I hope only to open up a long-forgotten way into the maze of this play, the amazing play of its imaginings, the magic imagery of its musing magus.

The best support for this view is that it gives the play a psychological relevance for me today.

It should by now be clear that I am using 'alchemy' to refer to a *medieval psychology of images which was basically aimed at soul-making* and not at the manipulation of materials in the interest of personal wealth or power.

Again, I believe we must be careful of literalism. It doesn't actually matter whether or not Prospero waved a wand and muttered an incantation and Ariel leapt out of the tree. The main thing to ask is: what is the psychological significance of this image? What we are interested in is how do we free the transcendent function from the binding forces of the negative mother complex?

We offered one answer to this by quoting from *Faust* where the hero must re-establish contact with the feminine principle from which he too, notoriously, was cut-off by going down to the realm of The Mothers. What he must do is to look at the dreaded thing until he can see its true nature and not be terrified of it. This is indeed a hero's journey. Jung described it in this fashion:

> . . . there lie at the root of the regressive longing, which Freud conceives as "infantile fixation" or the "incest wish", a specific value and a specific need which are made explicit in myths. It is precisely the strongest and best among men, the heroes, who give way to their regressive longing and purposely expose themselves to the danger of being devoured by the monster of the maternal abyss. But if a man is a hero, he is a hero because, in the final reckoning, he did not let the monster devour him, but subdued it, not once but many times. Victory over the collective psyche alone yields the true value — the capture of the hoard, the invincible weapon, the magic talisman, or whatever it may be that the myth deems most desirable. Anyone who identifies with the collective psyche — or in mythological terms, lets himself be devoured by the monster — and vanishes in it, attains the treasure that the dragon guards, but he does so in spite of himself and to his own greatest harm.
>
> (CW9,pt.1,p.170)

This is still rather vague. It says little about how the hero accomplishes this task. In his essay on the feeling function, James Hillman connects the "incestuous return" to the positive release of bound feeling: [59]

> When therapy speaks of the "incestuous return to the mother", it means going to the emotional depths where the feeling function lies bound. In this union with our own emotionality we are at our most intimate and weakest place, but often just here the feeling function has its roots.

The incestuous return alone can free feeling to function for me; my feelings here seem to be my own personal belongings, my treasure, as the myths would tell us, that is guarded by the mother-dragon of reptilian coldness and fiery passion, or by the witch herself who can turn us all back into dwarf tree-stumps, little birds a-twitter or just dumb stones. Incest, at this moment in the development of feeling, means allowing oneself to join with the darkest, bloodiest passions, the actual longings to be held and carried and caressed, the uninhibited rages and furies . . . It means going where the heart is, where we actually feel, even if in the fists, guts and genitals, rather than where the heart should be and how we ought to feel.

It is a common occurrence in the texts of the alchemists to find references to incest and emblems depicting it. For them it represented the *coniunctio* of opposites and thus a creative energy. Sterility was represented by a marriage of like and like; fertility by the marriage of opposites. One can see that both Jung and Hillman have been inspired by the alchemical style of personifying psychic experience. I believe that Shakespeare, in *The Tempest*, is completely at one with the alchemical psychology of his time and that this, rather than the pursuit of magical practices or summoning spirits, is the main content and framework of the play.

Prospero is inseparably, intimately, involved with Sycorax. She reflects his entire pre-exile relation to the unconscious. We could say that in one sense, she *is* his unconscious — except that she is much more than the personal unconscious. She represents all the feminine darkness and depth of the soul — which the spirit has tried to leave behind in its flight up the ordered, hierarchical pyramid towards the Supreme Godhead. She is, from the viewpoint of spirit, all that is clinging and encumbering, all that relates to the body and feeling, earthiness, uncertainty, ambiguity and multiplicity, the ever-changing play of the mysterious and the unknown which is life itself. And, as Prospero is her unconscious twin, he is also her unconscious lover and son. Prospero is the "freckled whelp hag-born — not honour'd with/ A human shape" whom Sycorax has "littered" on the island.

A protesting voice says, "Now you are imagining things! That makes Prospero, Caliban!"

Yes, we are imagining, or rather, allowing Shakespeare's *imaging* to take roots in our psyches and unfold. In this way we are giving the image its due recognition as the true voice of meaning. Images move the psyche, work within the psyche, bear fruit, ripen slowly into meaning.

Spirit would like sharp and clean definitions and precise meanings, fixed, if possible, into pure abstract form forever. It must learn to love and appreciate the soul's cloudiness, dreaminess and poignant sense of immanence. The soul, through the imagination, bodies forth images.

One such image is "a freckled whelp, hag-born — not honour'd with/ A human shape". What sort of monstrosity is this? Can we, like Jung, recognize the face that appears in the mirror? Or, are we embarrassed, outraged and distrustful of our Calibans? What manner of being is it who is the sole inhabitant of the island when Prospero arrives? Who is this low and foul creature?

6. Caliban

12. **Go to the woman who washes the sheets and do as she does.**

Whether Shakespeare consciously re-arranged the Elizabethan word 'canibal' to form the simple anagram 'Caliban', we do not know, but it is common to produce this as evidence of the intended inferior and barbaric nature of this strange creature. Shakespeare's contemporaries were perhaps closer to him than we are, but even they had their fantasies of the 'savage'.[60]

Caliban is the original 'wild man' of modern literature. It is easy to find sources that could have influenced Shakespeare's conception in sixteenth and seventeenth century accounts of the New World. First-hand reports of the American natives were being passionately discussed in England in the years immediately preceding the first known performance of *The Tempest*. There was also Florio's translation of Montaigne's essay, *Of the Canibales*, which was published in 1603. Montaigne had been very inspired by a friend of his who had spent twelve years living in the New World. There is a copy of this, according to Kermode,[61] which contains "what may be a genuine signature of Shakespeare". There are enough echoes of its language in the play to convince most scholars that Shakespeare was familiar with it. It is quite possible that Shakespeare actually lifted much material from it. But I feel that to consider Caliban merely as a representative of American Indians or African slaves is to miss his fundamental significance. Of course, he is the 'exploited native' and the 'dusky slave', *if* you see Prospero as a remote

Virginian plantation owner or a Renaissance duke. He is also the face of all the 'dark races' and citizens of under-developed countries. This is true. Nevertheless, we come closest to understanding Caliban if we see him in ourselves. This is, in fact, what Prospero is struggling to realize during the course of the play.

Let us turn to Caliban himself and to his relationship with Prospero. I have tried to show that Caliban is a completely natural outcome of Prospero's over-emphasis on the thinking and intuitive sides of his nature.

An astute director would have Caliban rising straight up "from the rock" in his first appearance on stage. For Caliban comes from the depths.

Son of Sycorax and the devil, born and bred on the island, Caliban is virtually synonymous with its entire psychological complex. Yet, in spite of being something "not honoured with human shape", Caliban is one of the most touching characters that Shakespeare ever created.

Caliban is certainly a child of his mother. But he is something else. He represents all the unlived life of Prospero, duke of Milan. All that Prospero has not lived out is brought into the open. Here is all that is sensually awake in life, as well as all that is filled with feeling. Within and behind the shadow lurk low and dark emotions: bitterness and envy, lust, hate and hurt-pride, demonic rage and crude sexuality.

We know from Prospero's speech to Ariel that Sycorax has "died". I understand this to mean the death of a certain constellation in the unconscious, because of a change in the conscious attitude. Prospero has begun to take cognisance of the feminine. He has had to. Caliban represents an eruption into consciousness of all the neglected unconscious contents. He is precisely that which Prospero is forced to come to terms with in himself, in order to become whole.

When we meet him in the play, Prospero has had twelve years of daily confrontation with the degraded, devalued inferior functions, personified in the figure of the brute, Caliban. One might say that Prospero has been an *apprentice* of Caliban for twelve years. In spite of the fact that he never yields a "kind answer" and that Miranda calls him a "villain" whom she does not "love to look on", he is absolutely essential:

> *Pros.*   But as 'tis
> We cannot miss him: he does make our fire,
> Fetch in our wood, and serves in offices
> That profit us.
>
> (I.ii.312-15)

Mark how Prospero reminds Miranda of Caliban's indispensibility. This 'monster' is Prospero's link with the earth. Without him, Prospero would never have survived. What a change has come in that duke of Milan, who "thus neglecting worldly ends" was "all dedicated/ To closeness and the bettering of [his] mind". *This* Prospero has 'come to his senses'.

And yet, Prospero still has all the trouble with Caliban that anyone has with the inferior function. It is "so close to the unconscious and remains so barbaric and inferior and undeveloped that it is naturally the weak spot in consciousness through which the figures of the unconscious can break in." [62]

> The inferior function is the ever-bleeding wound of the conscious personality, but through it the unconscious can always come in and so enlarge consciousness and bring forth a new attitude.[63]

Obviously, Prospero and Caliban do not get along well, but there is, all the same, a strong bond between them. And Caliban can hardly disguise his yearning to be accepted and recognized by Prospero. Prospero, in turn, recognizes Caliban's usefulness. He has learned to make the inferior function work for him. But he is unsure of Caliban and doesn't trust him. It is this that really hurts Caliban. Prospero does reject him, because he finds Caliban threatening. Caliban represents everything that Prospero has habitually refused to know about.

> *Pros.*   What, ho! slave! Caliban!
> Thou earth, thou! speak.
>
>   (I.ii.315-16)

And *what* speech emanates from this 'earth', this "salvage and deformed slave"!

> *Cal.*   As wicked dew as e'er my mother brush'd
>   With raven's feather from unwholesome fen
>   Drop on you both! a south-west blow on ye
>   And blister you all o'er!
>
>   (I.ii.323-26)

Prospero replies that, "For this, be sure, tonight thou shalt have cramps/ Side-stitches that shall pen thy breath up". Here, Prospero suggests a hidden connection between fantasy and illness. An evil wish, i.e. the wish that another being should physically suffer, returns to its owner as a similar physical torment. Caliban wishes that a pestilent wind should blow on Prospero and cause him to break out in blisters. The consequence of this wish is that Caliban himself will suffer from lack of breath and be "pinch'd/ As thick as honeycomb, each pinch more stinging/ Than bees that made 'em". (I.ii.330-333).

Caliban is in a ferment. His words pour out in an eloquent primitive poetry which shocks us — who have perhaps been expecting inarticulate fury. These are "the actual longings to be held and carried and caressed, the uninhibited rages and furies" which Hillman spoke of as lying at the emotional depths where feeling lies bound.

> Cal.   This island's mine, by Sycorax my mother,
> Which thou tak'st from me. When thou cam'st first,
> Thou strok'st me, and made much of me; would'st give me
> Water with berries in 't; and teach me how
> To name the bigger light, and how the less,
> That burn by day and night: and then I lov'd thee,
> And show'd thee all the qualities o' th' isle,
> The fresh springs, brine-pits, barren place and fertile:
> Curs'd be I that did so! All the charms
> Of Sycorax, toads, beetles, bats, light on you!
> For I am all the subjects that you have,
> Which first was mine own King: and here you sty me
> In this hard rock, whiles you do keep from me
> The rest o' th' island.
>
> (I.ii.334-346)

In his awareness of the location of fresh and salt water, fertile and unfertile ground, Caliban demonstrates the mode of the sensation function. Sensation is primarily sense-perception. It does not evaluate or judge, as do thinking and feeling. Like its conpensatory opposite, intuition, sensation is not subject to the laws of reason. Thus, Jung termed it an *irrational function*.[64]

We witness, in the exchanges between Prospero and Caliban, completely opposed ways of viewing the world.

> Pros.   Thou lying slave,
> Whom stripes may move, not kindness! I have us'd thee,
> Filth as thou art, with human care; and lodg'd thee
> In mine own cell, till thou did'st seek to violate
> The honour of my child.
>
> Cal.   Oho, Oho! would't had been done!
> Thou did'st prevent me; I had peopled else
> This isle with Calibans.
>
> (I.ii.346-353)

Caliban laughs in Prospero's face. If Prospero had not prevented him, Caliban assures us, he would have violated the honour of Miranda and "peopled else this isle with Calibans". In other words, the inferior function, if not made conscious, would consume everything else — it would eat up the other functions completely, like cancer. In the words of psychology, if Prospero had not consciously prohibited the incest desire, *as mirrored in Caliban*, the integrity of his soul would have been destroyed or severely damaged. Caliban represents the open and naked expression of the incest desire. In an ordered, tribal society the incest taboo is collectively reinforced, such that little is left to the individual. In fact, as Robert Stein writes:[65]

> The elaborate precautions taken by 'primitives' to prevent a violation
> of the incest taboo suggest the intensity of the incest desire is too strong
> to be left to individual responsibility.

This last, however, is exactly the situation in which Prospero and his daughter find themselves. They can not rely on the "elaborate precautions" of social conventions and rituals, because they are outside society. Repression is also, obviously, not the answer. Making the incest prohibition a *conscious* thing, introduces a moral conflict, but it avoids the internal split between love and sex which is a consequence of the repression of incest desire. As far as I understand Stein's thinking on this, repression is the outcome of the disintegration of those social forms which enable parent, child and siblings to experience instinctual sexuality without guilt. This is largely the situation in our own day, where the incest taboo is no longer dealt with consciously, but has fallen into the unconscious and functions autonomously.[66]

Earlier, in the discussion of Sycorax, we spoke of the "incestuous return" and the great value given to this by myth. There we spoke of the hero who gives way to regressive longings and purposely exposes himself to the danger of being devoured by the monster of the maternal abyss. We saw how the hero becomes a hero through his victory over the collective psyche. We compared Prospero to the hero in his obvious confrontation with the negative mother complex in the form of Sycorax (and her island). Now there is a development. A further differentiation must take place. Miranda, who is, I feel, the carrier of soul, or the anima, must be separated out from the negative feminine and distinguished from the wholly unconscious morass of inferior feeling, personified by Caliban. She must face instinctual sexuality, but also be protected from violation. In this way her consciousness will develop, a consciousness of soul, a soul-consciousness. Remember Prospero's comforting words to Miranda: "I have done nothing but in care of thee,/ Of thee, my dear one; thee, my daughter, who/ Art ignorant of what thou art" (I.ii.16-18). We are watching the gradual shift of standpoint. Spirit has begun to value soul and to turn towards it in appreciation rather than away from it in irritation. As Prospero becomes more familiar with the contents of the unconscious, these contents themselves undergo change. We see yet another manifestation of the transcendent function.

This continual process of getting to know the counterposition in the unconscious I have called the transcendent function, because the confrontation of conscious (rational) data with those that are unconscious (irrational) necessarily results in a modification of standpoint. But an alteration is possible only if the existence of the 'outer' is admitted, at least to the point of taking conscious cognizance of it.

(CW.14.p.200)

It is my hunch that Caliban embodies much of this Other which must be admitted into consciousness by Prospero. He, himself, however, seems nearly impervious to all attempts to change him. In this respect, he bears an extraordinary resemblance to the character of the shadow, as Jung describes it, with all its inferiorities and weaknesses.

Although, with insight and good will, the shadow can to some extent be assimilated into the conscious personality, experience shows that there are certain features which offer the most obstinate resistance to moral control and prove almost impossible to influence. Those resistances are usually bound up with *projections*, which are not recognized as such, and their recognition is a moral achievement beyond the ordinary. While some traits peculiar to the shadow can be recognized without too much difficulty as one's own personal qualities, in this case both insight and good will are unavailing because the cause of the emotion appears to lie, beyond all possibility of doubt, in the *other person*. No matter how obvious it may be to the neutral observer that it is a matter of projections, there is little hope that the subject will perceive this himself. He must be willing to withdraw his emotionally-toned projections from their object.

(CW.9.pt.1.p.9)

Or, as Shakespeare puts it in the following speech (which, like Dryden, I am inclined to give to Prospero, not Miranda):

> (*Mir.*)   Abhorred slave,
> Which any print of goodness wilt not take,
> Being capable of all ill! I pitied thee,
> Took pains to make thee speak, taught thee each hour
> One thing or other: when thou did'st not, savage,
> Know thine own meaning, but would'st gabble like
> A thing most brutish, I endow'd thy purposes
> With words that made them known. But thy vile race,
> Though thou didst learn, had that in't which good natures
> Could not abide to be with; therefore wast thou
> Deservedly confin'd into this rock,
> Who hadst deserv'd more than a prison.

(I.ii.353-64)

The education and assimilation of the shadow and the inferior function(s) is a slow and hard task. Twelve years' work in assimilating the *auxiliary* functions alone is not unusual.[67] Above and beyond that, the work involved in bringing up the inferior function is enormous. Giving it attention is always an awkward situation for the superior function.

> *Cal.*   You taught me language; and my profit on't
> Is, I know how to curse. The red plague rid you
> For learning me your language!

And so, Prospero sends Caliban away with threats reminiscent of Sycorax (which shows how close he still is to her). Caliban bows to Prospero's authority because he sees that it could control even his mother's god: Setebos. Yet, Prospero shows little affection for him, and Caliban winces under this harsh rejection. And, as Caliban leaves the stage, Ariel now reappears, "invisible, playing and singing", with Ferdinand following.

> *Ariel's song*
>
> *Come unto these yellow sands,*
> *And then take hands:*
> *Courtsied when you have and kiss'd*
> *The wild waves whist:*
> *Foot it featly here and there,*
> *And sweet sprites bear*
> *The burthen. Hark, hark.*
>
> (Burthen dispersedly.) *Bow-wow.*
>
> *Ari.*   *The watch dogs bark:*
>
> (Burthen dispersedly.) *Bow-wow.*
>
> *Ari.*   *Hark, hark! I hear*
> *The strain of strutting chanticleer*
>
> *Cry* — (Burthen dispersedly.) *Cock a diddle dow.*
>
> (I.ii.376-389)

Just before Prospero called Caliban, he sent Ariel off, with the words, "Go make thy self like a nymph o' th' sea:/ Be subject to/ No sight but thine and mine; invisible/ To every eyeball else". Now, Ariel returns, transformed into a nymph. Mercurius, as the alchemists tell us, is both male and female. After a manifestation as spiritual fire and lightning in the storm, Ariel appears as a female creature of the sea, seductively drawing Ferdinand with poetry and music. The song is an invitation to the dance, to take hands, courtsy, and kiss the wild waves' whist (silence). The mention of yellow sands is a solar image, as is the "strutting chanticleer" and its "cock a diddle dow". These images all serve to introduce the young man who is suffering from the delusion that he is shipwrecked, Ferdinand. Ariel, as anima, is working a charm on Ferdinand with the magnetizing music of the soul. Ferdinand, otherwise a member of the patriarchal, mainland consciousness, represents the spirit awakening to the *quality* of soul.

7. Full Fathom Five Thy Father Lies

13. As coral grows under water, &, exposed to the air, gets hard, so also the stone.

There is surely no more mysterious and enchanting song in the English language than that which Ariel sings to Ferdinand. The young prince is completely captivated. He forgets everything and follows wherever it leads him.

Fer. Where should this music be? i' th' air or the 'arth?
It sounds no more: and sure it waits upon
Some god o' th' island. Sitting on a bank,
Weeping again the King my father's wrack,
This music crept by me upon the waters,
Allaying both their fury and my passion
With its sweet air: thence I have follow'd it,
Or it hath drawn me rather. But 'tis gone.
No, it begins again.

Ariel's song.

Full fathom five thy father lies;
*   Of his bones are coral made;*
Those are pearls that were his eyes:
*   Nothing of him that doth fade,*
But doth suffer a sea-change

> *Into something rich and strange.*
> *Sea-nymphs hourly ring his knell:*

Burthen: *Ding-dong.*

Ari.   *Hark! now I hear them, — Ding-dong, bell.*

Fer.   The ditty does remember my drown'd father.
This is no mortal business, nor no sound
That the earth owes:- I hear it now above me.

(I.ii.390-410)

Ariel is telling Ferdinand, if he could understand, that his father is not drowned; he is undergoing a "sea-change". The Father is the ruling principle of consciousness. He is the King, the incarnation of the patriarchal Logos, the masculine dominant. In the highest sense, he is God, the Father. But the Father God inevitably becomes a notorious tyrant, a hard and harsh despot, ruling by repression, who outlaws soul and imagination, who glories in power, a cynical brute of pure reason, devoid of depth and creative darkness because he constantly rejects his own feminine deeps. It is this amplified image of the old king, the negative senex figure of sterile authority and hardened arteries, stony face and rigid rule, which is undergoing transformation. In this play on alchemical imagery Ariel sings his sea-change into something rich and strange, chemical-poetic coagulations of sea-stuff, eyes born of oysters, bones of glowing, living stone. This is five fathoms down, or up, on the fifth level, the level of the fifth, the transcendent function. Sea-nymphs hourly ring his knell. But he does not fade or die, he is suffering a sea-change. In other words, he has returned to the Great Mother, and in her waters, the sea of the vast collective unconscious, he is being worked upon, being given a new body, a body born of the sea, a body of images, eyes for deep-sea-ing into psyche's ocean.

Ferdinand is, of course, the bearer of this change, though it is pre-figured by Prospero's own radical change. Ferdinand, moreover, is the Prince who will be the New King. Now, still fresh from his recent immersion in the waters, he is led by Ariel/Mercurius up to the magician's cell where his soul-mate waits.

Pros.   The fringed curtains of thine eyes advance,
And say what thou seest yond.

Mir.   What is 't? a spirit?
Lord, how it looks about! Believe me, sir,
It carries a brave form. But 'tis a spirit.

14.

Pros.   No, wench; it eats and sleeps and hath such senses
         As we have, such. This gallant which thou seest
         Was in the wrack; and, but he's something stain'd
         With grief (that's beauty's canker) thou mightest call him
         A goodly person: he hath lost his fellows,
         And strays about to find 'em.

Mir.   I might call him
         A thing divine; for nothing natural
         I ever saw so noble.

Pros.   (*Aside*) It goes on, I see.
         As my soul prompts it.

                                                        (I.ii.411-423)

Following the promptings of soul, Prospero has introduced the two young
people and they have fallen immediately in love. This is not simply Romeo
and Juliet over again. Miranda, more than Caliban, more than Ariel, even
more than Prospero, is the embodiment of soul. Grief may be the cancer
of beauty, but beauty, and by this I mean true soul-beauty, is the flower,
the mystic Rose, which grows from the dark soul-soil of conscious suffering.

I feel that students of *The Tempest* pass too quickly over the fact of Prospero's
exile from Milan. Of course, we all read our own stories into the play, and
I may be giving overmuch importance to this, but I feel that Prospero has
undergone tremendous suffering during his exile; suffering not only through
the experience of rejection and abandonment, of loss and separation, but
through the experience of confrontation with the darkness within himself,
the self-doubt and the gradual awakening to the realization that his destiny
is *his*. It is a measure of his, and Shakespeare's, greatness, that he accepts
his fate and does not curse the gods or the heavens and turn embittered
and obsessed with revenge.

Miranda has accompanied her father on this voyage of self-exploration
and realization. She has been a witness to his torment and pain and his
great love. This has been her true education. That and the island. The spirits.
The music. The elemental energies. The unfathomable, all-surrounding sea.

Ferdinand is not an initiate of all this. He is the son of a king of power.
He comes from the court and the mainland. His background is everything
that conspired to cast Prospero (and Miranda) into exile, all that Prospero
neglected to relate with, all that he undervalued and ignored.

Now the two children of the opposing (or apparently opposing) powers
have met. But being in love is not enough. Prospero wants to somehow
to ensure that they will make a true marriage. He especially is determined
to test Ferdinand's steadfastness and endurance, as his next words
demonstrate:

Pros.   (*Aside*) They are both in either's pow'rs: but this
            swift business
            I must uneasy make, lest too light winning
            Make the prize light. (*To Fer.*) One word more;
               I charge thee
            That thou attend me: thou dost here usurp
            The name thou ow'st not; and hast put thyself
            Upon this island as a spy, to win it
            From me, the lord on't.

When Ferdinand objects and Miranda begins to plead for him, Prospero
pretends great wrath —

Pros.   Follow me.
            Speak not you for him: he's a traitor. Come;
            I'll manacle thy neck and feet together.
            Sea-water shalt thou drink; thy food shall be
            The fresh-brook mussels, wither'd roots, and husks
            Wherein the acorn cradled. Follow.

                                              (I.ii.463-7)

Ferdinand is unable to disobey — immobilized by the magician's stronger
will and 'charmed from moving' when he draws his sword. Prospero is
'acting': a paranoid, half-crazy, jealous father. Secretly, he is joyful. The
prince is already so devoted to Miranda that he will gladly suffer prison
for her sake. Prospero promises to manacle the prince's neck to his feet —
symbolically linking the above to the below. And he threatens to feed the
young man on acorn husks and roots — food traditionally associated with
the pig, the animal sacred to the most ancient of goddesses.

Underneath this show of tetchy fury and paranoia, Prospero can barely
hide his happiness. Already he loves Ferdinand as though he were his own
son. But he will not show it. Not yet.

15.

Notes to Part I

All quotations from *The Tempest* are from the Arden edition (Kermode) 1954, 1979.

1. Elizabeth Sewell: *The Orphic Voice*. Routledge & Kegan Paul, London, 1961, p. 55.
2. James Hillman: *Peaks and Vales — The Soul/Spirit Distinction as a Basis for the Difference between Psychotherapy and Spiritual Discipline* in *Puer Papers*, ed. J. Hillman, Spring Publications, Dallas, 1979.
3. S. T. Coleridge: *Lectures on Shakespeare*. Section I.
4. Hillman: op. cit. p. 56.
5. King James VI (of Scotland, later James I of England): *Daemonologie, in forme of a Dialogue*. Edinburgh, 1597, p. xiii. ff.
6. All quotations from the Fian affair are from King James VI: *Newes from Scotland*. London, 1591, p. 28-9.
7. I am indebted to Ronald Laing for calling my attention to Bacon's early formulations of the scientific method. An excellent and chilling account of where this method of 'scientific objectivity' has led some of us can be found in Laing's recent book, *The Voice of Experience*. Allen Lane, 1982.
8. Frances Yates: *Shakespeare's Last Plays*. Routledge & Kegan Paul, London, 1975, p. 95.
9. Frances Yates: *The Occult Philosophy in the Elizabethan Age*. R. & K. P., 1979.
10. F. Yates: *S.L.P.*, p. 118.
11. The Image of the Hexagram, CHEN — the Arousing. *I-Ching*. Richard Wilhelm translation. Routledge & Kegan Paul, 1951, p. 296., Vol. 1.
12. Wm. Shakespeare: *Anthony and Cleopatra*. I.ii.144-146.
13. R. D. Laing: *Do You Love Me?* Pantheon. New York, 1976, p. 70.

14. "I'll warrant him for drowning . . ." etc. = 'I would authorize his pardon from having to be drowned, even if this were a weak and leaky vessel.' To support this view the Arden edition suggests, following Abbott, that 'for' in this context can be equivalent to 'against'.

15. Jung says: "In accordance with the principle of compensation which runs through the whole of nature, every psychic development, whether individual or collective, possesses an optimum which, when exceeded, produces an enantiodromia, that is, turns into its opposite. Compensatory tendencies emanating from the unconscious may be noted, even during the approach to the critical turning-point, though if consciousness persists in its course, they are completely repressed. The stirrings in the darkness necessarily seem like a devilish betrayal of spiritual development." CW.13.p.245. CW = *The Collected Works of C. G. Jung*. Trans. by R. F. C. Hull, Routledge and Kegan Paul, London.

16. *Jonah* — 1:4 (King James version).

17. See James Hillman: *Revisioning Psychology*. Harper, New York & London, 1975, for a description of literalism, pp. 11, 46, 136, 150, 174, etc.

18. Marie Louise von Franz: *Interpretation of Fairy Tales*. p. 89, Spring Publications, Dallas, 1978.

19. Here, I am in total disagreement with Martin Lings who says that "there can be no doubt that it is she [Miranda] who represents the Spirit and Ferdinand the soul", p. 111 in *Shakespeare in the Light of Sacred Art*. George Allen and Unwin, 1966. Lings' book is otherwise delightful and full of valuable insights. But, on this count, I feel that he is trying to force the figures in the play into preconceived moulds to fit his theory — rather than listening to what the characters have to say and allowing them to reveal their function.

20. G. Wilson Knight: *The Crown of Life*. Methuen & Co., London, 1947, p. 28 (from "Myth and Miracle" 1929).

21. For a further exploration of soul as psychological understanding see J. Hillman: *Revisioning Psychology* as well as his two very fine expositions "Anima I & II" in Spring 1973 and 1974. Spring Publ., New York.

22. *The Letters of John Keats*. Reeves & Turner, London, 1895, letter of April, 1819, p. 326.

23. Ivy has its roots in the ground and draws its sustenance from there and the air and sunlight. It uses a support upon which to climb, but it does not "suck" nourishment from the supporting tree.

24. C. G. Jung: *The Interpretation of Visions*. Spring, 1960.

25. Goethe: *Faust* Pt. 1. from the Penguin transl. by P. Wayne, p. 56.

26. Nagarjuna: *Mulamadhyamakakarika XXV*. 19-20. The Mahasiddhas,

or Great Realised Ones, were Buddhist practitioners in Mediaeval India, from all walks of life. Collections of their life stories exist today only in Tibetan. *Samsara* is traditionally regarded as the vicious cycle of transmigration. It is characterized by suffering and arises out of ignorance. *Nirvana*, in its limited sense, means 'cessation from suffering', but in its highest sense means 'enlightenment', i.e. cessation of ignorance and the arising of compassion and skilful means to work with the bewilderment of sentient beings.

27. Frances Yates: *Giordano Bruno and the Hermetic Tradition*. Routledge & Kegan Paul, London, 1964, p. 148.
28. From Dee's preface to Billingsey's *The Elements of . . . Euclide*. London, 1570.
29. Peter French: *John Dee — The World of an Elizabethan Magus*. Routledge & Kegan Paul, London, 1972, p. 106.
30. Ibid. p. 115.
31. C. G. Jung: *Man and His Symbols*. Aldus Books, London, 1964, p. 61.
32. Jung: *Psychological Types*. Routledge & Kegan Paul, London, 1925, p.508.
33. Op. cit. p. 510.
34. James Hillman in *The Feeling Function* p. 80 in *Jung's Typology* by von Franz and Hillman, Spring, N.Y., 1971.
35. Op. cit. p. 107.
36. Ibid. p. 111-112.
37. Frances Yates: *SLP*, p. 120.
38. G. Wilson Knight: op. cit. p. 254.
39. Ibid. p. 232.
40. I have here used the *Folio* punctuation as it gives a much more startling and poetically true image — of Ferdinand leaping overboard with flaming hair and fingers.
41. C. G. Jung: *Psychological Commentary on Kundalini Yoga*. Lecture One, 1932. Published in *Spring*, 1975, Zurich, p. 11ff.
42. Aristophanes: *Peace*. 394.
43. W. F. Otto: *The Homeric Gods*. Thames & Hudson, London, 1954, p. 114.
44. See James Hillman: *Revisioning Psychology*. pp. 205ff.
45. R. Lopez-Pedraza: *Hermes and his Children*. Spring Publ., Zurich, 1977, p. 5.
46. *Theatrum Chemicum* Vol. IV. (1659) as quoted in C. G. Jung, CW.13, p. 218.
47. Marsilio Ficino: (1489) *Opera Omnia*. Basilae, 1576, p. 1747, as quoted in D. P. Walker: *Spiritual and Demonic Magic from Ficino to Campanella*. London, 1958, p. 23.

48. Colin Still: *The Timeless Theme*. Ivor Nicolson & Watson, London, 1936, p. 212.
49. Kermode in The Arden edition of *The Tempest*. 1964, p. x1.
50. Robert Graves: *The White Goddess*. Faber & Faber, London, 1971, p. 426.
51. Marie Louise von Franz: *Shadow and Evil in Fairy Tales*. Spring Publ., 1974, p. 104-105.
52. *C. G. Jung Letters*. ed. by Gerhard Adler. Routledge & Kegan Paul, London, 1973, Vol. 1, p. 52. (Letter to Keyserling, 25 August 1928.)
53. Marie Louise von Franz: *A Psychological Interpretation of The Golden Ass of Apuleius*. Spring Publ., 1970, VI. 1.
54. Ibid. II. 8.
55. Von Franz: *Shadow & Evil* etc., p. 106.
56. *C. G. Jung Letters*. Vol. 1, p. 41. (Letter to O. Schmitz, 26 May 1923.)
57. Goethe: *Faust pt. 2*. Tr. by Philip Wayne. Penguin, 1959, p. 76.
58. C. J. Sisson: *The Magic of Prospero*. Shakespeare Survey Vol. 11, Cambridge, 1958, p. 74.
59. J. Hillman: in his essay, *The Feeling Function* in *Jung's Typology*. Von Franz & Hillman, Spring Publ., N.Y., 1971, p. 116.
60. See for example: R. Berheimer: *Wild Men in the Middle Ages*. Harvard University Press, 1952.
61. Kermode. Arden edition of *The Tempest*. Appendix C, p. 145.
62. Von Franz: *Jung's Typology*. p. 54.
63. Ibid.
64. "In so far as sensation is an elementary phenomenon, it is something absolutely given, something that, in contrast to thinking and feeling, is not subject to the laws of reason. I therefore term it an *irrational* function, although reason contrives to assimilate a great number of sensations into rational associations." C. G. Jung: *Psychological Types*, p. 587
65. R. Stein: *Incest and Human Love*. Penguin Books, Maryland, 1974, p. 41.
66. Ibid. I feel that Stein's book is a major contribution to a very confused area within psychology.
67. See von Franz's discussion of this in her essay on the inferior function in *Jung's Typology*, p. 54ff.

16.

PART II

MAINLAND CONSCIOUSNESS

Western man has no need of more superiority over nature, whether outside or inside. He has both in devilish perfection. What he lacks is conscious recognition of his inferiority to the nature around and within him. He must learn that he may not do exactly as he wills. If he does not learn this, his own nature will destroy him.

— C. G. Jung. CW.11.par.870

1. Mainland Consciousness

17. He who tries to penetrate into the Philosophical Rose Garden without a key, resembles a man who wants to walk without feet.

In Act I we heard how Prospero, Duke of Milan, had, through being "transported/ And rapt in secret studies", lost his dukedom to his brother, Antonio, who, taking advantage of Prospero's "neglect" of "worldly ends", carried out a coup d'état and banished Prospero and his baby daughter in a "rotten carcase of a butt" on the open seas. We heard how the boat brought them to the island where Sycorax, the witch, had imprisoned the spirit, Ariel, in a cloven pine and where, after her death, Caliban, her son by the devil, was reigning as his "own King". We heard how, at first, Prospero "made much" of Caliban, taught him language and even housed him in his cell; then, finding that "any print of goodness" would not take on Caliban, kept him enslaved by his superior powers. We heard how Prospero freed Ariel from his twelve year long confinement and became his new master. We watched as Prospero, with the aid of Ariel, raised the storm and magnetically brought the ship with his enemies on it straight into his field of power. We witnessed the enchantment of Miranda's first meeting with Ferdinand, the son of King Alonso, one of Prospero's chief enemies. The first act ended in a magical, other-world reverie, hardly marred by Prospero's gruff pretence of irritable suspicion.

The second act opens with a total change of mood. The stark contrast of the poisonous-minded members of the Court Party, all manners and hidden daggers, brings us up short. We remember them from the scene on the storm-tossed ship in the play's opening. Here they are then: Alonso, sunk in a state of shocked despair; Antonio and Sebastian, arrogant, cynical, ruthless; Gonzalo, awkwardly maternal. Apart from Gonzalo, these are the men who have usurped Prospero's dukedom. Looked at in terms of the psyche, they represent extraverted thinking and intuition, calculating and opportunist, with severe denial of the introverted life, as represented by early Prospero. They champion that consciousness in Western civilization which is furthest from the intimate relationship with nature and soul and the feminine.

If early Prospero is said to have *neglected* worldly ends, then these men could be said to *worship* them. They, in their turn, have neglected both spirit and soul, though in a sense we could say that they represent the masculine intellect at its most crass — in its domination over feeling. They embody the dominant ideals and attitudes of Western civilization, which was — and still is — based on masculine primacy and feminine inferiority.

Peter Redgrove and Penelope Shuttle in their excellent study of the mysteries and mystifications of menstruation give the following description of *man's* idea of love: "self-righteous, territorial, wrathful, phallic, chauvinist, bellicose, with man the lord of creation and a Father the lord of heaven and earth."[1]

We might add that men have consistently created societies which fundamentally are projections of their ideal of the heroic ego. And the shadow side of this heroic ego is tyrannical, arrogant, unforgiving, unfeeling, unimaginative and imperialistic.

Prospero turned away from any involvement with this world, searching within for a deeper meaning. However, by so doing, he ignored the very real danger of the power-complex and barely escaped a tragic end. This is the true crux of the play. How can I be *in* the world but not *of* it?

Antonio, Sebastian and Alonso are not simply the villains of the play. They represent the power-complex of the masculine psyche which Prospero has ignored and covered over with a shadow. To be truly whole Prospero must relate to this power-complex, both internally and externally. He must come to terms with this fierce, territory-mad bull. Instead of covering his eyes and pretending it is not there, he must confront it, recognizing its lethal power. However, he isn't obliged to let it gore him or trample him into the dirt. Like the Cretan bull-dancers of ancient Knossos, he can *transcend* it, taking it by the horns and somersaulting over it, out of danger, to land on its back — where he can ride it. Transposed to the realm of psyche, this awe-inspiring feat is what Shakespeare is demonstrating in this, his last message to mankind. He shows us the true magician: he who is a master of himself.

Thus, if the island represents the autonomous complex of the neglected feminine, the domain of the mother-goddess, then *the mainland itself* is the stronghold of masculine consciousness, the supremacy of the father-god. And now, fortune and Prospero's Art have brought the representatives of the mainland to the island.

Gonzalo, the honest counsellor, attempts to console King Alonso with the fact that they have cause for joy, since they have escaped drowning. But the King is inaccessible in his depression, believing his son is lost. Gonzalo, on the whole, comes across as a feeling-type and thus outside what I have called the mainland consciousness. Even though he is not completely in touch with his feeling function, he is, nonetheless, far more so than either Antonio or Sebastian.

Adr.	The air breathes upon us here most sweetly.
Seb.	As if it had lungs, and rotten ones.
Ant.	Or as 'twere perfum'd by a fen.

(II.i.45-47)

Sebastian and Antonio do not see the same island as Adrian and Gonzalo. Their perception is coloured by their fantasy of the feminine, which the island represents. Colin Still says it this way:[2] "The Island presents the aspect of Purgatory, of Elysium or Paradise, according to the psychological state of the percipient." I would agree, merely adding that the psychological state of the percipient is mainly determined by his relationship to psyche, since psyche is happy, harpy, hideous, delightful, seductive, witch-like, petulant, wise, sullen, furious or enfuriating, depending on the kind of attention given to her.

Adrian, earlier, has remarked that "though the island seem to be desert . . . uninhabitable and almost inaccessible . . . it must needs be of subtle, tender and delicate temperance." This insight is met with derision by Antonio and Sebastian. The conversion continues:

Gon.	Here is everything advantageous to life.
Ant.	True; save means to live.
Seb.	Of that there's none, or little.
Gon.	How lush and lusty the grass looks! how green!
Ant.	The ground, indeed, is tawny.
Seb.	With an eye of green in 't.
Ant.	He misses not much.

Seb.   No; he doth but mistake the truth totally.

                                                        (II.i.48-55)

This last line is amazing. Sebastian simply denies Gonzalo's perception any truth whatsoever. Next, when Gonzalo muses over the miraculous state of their garments which appear fresh and new-dyed, rather than stained with salt water, Antonio snidely jibes: "If but one of his pockets could speak, would it not say he lies?"

Gonzalo, however, will not back down: "Methinks our garments are now as fresh as when we put them on first in Afric, at the marriage of the King's fair daughter Claribel to the King of Tunis." This spurs Adrian (II.i.71-2) to say: "Tunis was never grac'd before with such a paragon/ to their queen."

The following section of the play — an apparent muddle of irrelevance — begins with a strange remark Gonzalo blurts in answer to Adrian's claim above —

Gon.   No since widow Dido's time.

— and continues with a series of frantic witticisms by Antonio and Sebastian, as though Gonzalo had inadvertently let the cat out of the bag, and they were hoping to obscure it in a dust-cloud of words.

Ant.   Widow! a pox o' that! How came that widow in?
              Widow Dido!

                                                        (II.ii.74-5)

What is the 'cat', then? First, listen to one Shakespearian scholar, Frank Kermode:

> This line begins a series of apparently trivial allusions to the theme of Dido and Aeneas which has never been properly explained; if they are to be taken at their face value, one must allow that Lytton Strachey's strictures on this scene are perfectly justified. He speaks of 'the dreary puns and interminable conspiracies' as an indication of Shakespeare's fatigue. But we must not take them at their face value. *The Tempest* is far from being a loosely built play; and nowhere in Shakespeare, not even in his less intensive work, is there anything resembling the apparent irrelevances of lines 73-97. It is a possible inference that our frame of reference is badly adjusted, or incomplete, and that an understanding of this passage will modify our image of the whole play.[3]

I feel that Kermode is right in suspecting that our frame of reference is badly adjusted. Together with Homer and Dante, Virgil is one of the great poets of all time, and Shakespeare would have been well acquainted with

6

18.

his epic of the founding of Rome, the *Aeneid*. Like Shakespeare, Virgil recapitulated much of the Western myth of its history in his writing, borrowing freely from Homer, for example, in the story of the Trojan war and Aeneas' flight from Troy. Thus, the *Aeneid* participates in and carries on the myths at the heart of the Western psyche. The myth of the founding of Rome, with all its implications for the development of civilization in the West, would have been of much interest to a mind like Shakespeare's. Thus, it is not an uncrafted *non-sequitur* which slips into the master bard's speech here. It merely appears as an irrelevance. In fact, it is a 'Jungian-slip', a funny-smelling archetypal bubble bursting into the all-too-suspiciously-pure air of the thinking function from the fertile depths of myth below.

The cat in the bag is surely the suppressed and devalued feminine. Listen to this indictment of our civilization by a contemporary woman — in her book, *A Psychological Interpretation of the Golden Ass of Apuleius,* Marie-Louise von Franz is talking of the effort of the feminine to push up from where the late Greek civilization had buried it. She quotes many examples from Apuleius' novel. But, she says,

> It does not appear only in this novel, but also, for instance, in the beautiful mythology of the story of Dido and Aeneas in Virgil: Venus behind Dido, trying to bring up the feminine principle, and then politics cutting the whole thing apart, and Dido destroying herself by committing suicide because she is a victim of politics. The gods decided that Rome had to be founded so that Aeneas could not stay forever in the happy land of Carthage, and the love affair which the gods themselves had arranged could not go on. For the sake of politics the feminine was destroyed and roams about as a suicidal, unredeemed ghost in the beautiful scene where Aeneas goes into the underworld and sees her and she turns away, still resentful of what he had done to her. It is, therefore, not only in our novel that this problem comes up, but in many attempts, and it always ends tragically and leads nowhere.[4]

Notice that von Franz says that the feminine was destroyed. And — "roaming about the *underworld* as a suicidal, unredeemed ghost"? Would it not be more appropriate to say the "unconscious", or better, the "collective unconscious", instead of the underworld? For this is the case, just as much now as in Shakespeare's time, perhaps even more so. In Shakespeare's time there were still many women who were active members of "Hera's Colleges", whether or not they held union cards. It is estimated that millions of them were executed as witches in his era.

> In the Middle Ages it has been estimated that nine million women were burned as witches for exercising their natural crafts of midwifery,

hypnotism, healing, dowsing, dream-study and sexual fulfilment. They
were persecuted and burned by the Christian Church of that time, who
wished only men to have power and ability, by men worshipping a male
trinity.[5]

Shakespeare was very aware of this phenomenon, if we are to give any
weight to the numerous (and knowledgeable) references to witchcraft in
his work. He could not have helped also being aware of the counterforces
arraigned *against* the practice of such natural crafts. Shakespeare obviously
did not share King James' view that all witches were bad, but he kept his
ideas to himself. Everyone knew how James had tortured and burned Doctor
Fian and made mincemeat of the Berwick witches in 1591[6] King James
(the VI of Scotland and I of England) feared witches like the plague. Nowhere
has the attitude of James I been put more succinctly than in this passage
by William Perkins in his work on witchcraft in 1616:[7]

> It is a principle of the Law of nature, holden for a grounded truth in
> all Countries and Kingdoms, among all people in every age; that the
> traytor who is an enemie to the State, and rebelleth against his lawfull
> Prince, should be put to death; now the most notorious traytor and rebel
> that can be, is the Witch. For she renounceth God himself, the King
> of Kings, she leaves the society of his Church and people, she bindeth
> herself in league with the devil.

This is exactly what von Franz is referring to when she speaks of Dido,
as the "victim of politics". If women's mysteries became 'ugly', 'obscene',
and 'disorderly', why didn't men look in their hearts for the answer? After
all, these women were their wives, mothers, daughters, aunts and
grandmothers. Why? Because they had invalidated the heart. Then, how
logical to say that the witch is the "most notorious traytor and rebel that
can be" because "she renounceth God himself, the King of Kings". And
what women would not be tempted (at least) to parody the male superiority
and thumb their noses at the "society of his Church"? Even if they were
quietists, they must have been acutely aware of the injustice being perpetrated
against their sisters in God's name. Thus, Christ was crucified anew, in
women.

What then happened to the feminine side of men? It too was degraded,
ridiculed, punished and tormented. It too went underground. Thus,
Gonzalo's Jungian slip and Antonio's immediate rejoinder:

> *Ant.*   Widow! a pox o' that! How came that widow in?
>   Widow Dido!

But the Widow has come in — she is mentioned no less than six times

in this short section. Her image rushes in — hair streaming, clothes covered
in blood, crying and groaning. But no one wants to acknowledge her. Even
her name makes them jump — like cowboys having their boots shot at.
It is as though the very mention of a female survivor of a syzygy strikes
terror into their hearts. It is an unconscious reaction — to cover the raw
wound and begin talking of something quite innocuous: that Gonzalo is
so stupid as to think that Tunis and Carthage are the same city, that
everything he says is either impossible or ridiculous:

Ant.   His word is more than the miraculous harp.

Seb.   He hath rais'd the wall, and houses too.

Ant.   What impossible matter will he make easy next?

Seb.   I think he will carry this island home in his pocket, and give
         it his son for an apple.

Ant.   And, sowing the kernels of it in the sea, bring forth more
         islands.

Gon.   Ay.

                                                          (II.i.83-90)

Widow Dido momentarily disappears, as the image changes to the walls
of Thebes magically rising to the music of Amphion's harp. And Thebes
now metamorphoses into an island which becomes an apple. It is significant
that in the attempt to make a fool out of Gonzalo, Sebastian hits upon the
image of the apple. In Western tradition the apple has always been linked
with Eve and the Garden of Eden, as the fruit of the tree which gave
knowledge of good and evil. Linking the island to this fruit of sacred
knowledge, shows that even Sebastian is aware on some level that the island
is no ordinary place. Of course, he means it as nonsense, but he is
unconsciously speaking the truth. No doubt, given the chance, Gonzalo
would "carry the island home in his pocket" (take the essence or fruit of
the experience of the adventure back home with him) and "give it his son
for an apple". And, "sowing the kernels of it in the sea" (distributing
knowledge to his friends and relatives), "bring forth more islands".

After more berating and accusations, Sebastian reveals that he holds the
King to blame for *both* the loss of Ferdinand and Claribel — for if Alonso
had not married Claribel off to an African, none of them would ever have
gone on this voyage in the first place. King Alonso groans for the anguish
he finds himself in but cannot express.

Alon.   Prithee, peace.

Seb.   You were kneel'd to, and importun'd otherwise,
           By all of us; and the fair soul herself
           Weigh'd between loathness and obedience, at
           Which end o' th' beam should bow. We have lost your son,
           I fear, forever: Milan and Naples have
           Mo'widows in them of this business' making
           Than we bring men to comfort them:
           The fault's your own.

Alon.   So is the dear'st o' th' loss.

                                            (II.ii.123-131)

Like the butterfly unfolding from its chrysalis, another kind of truth emerges, a more feminine truth, which distinguishes itself from Sebastian's (II.i.55) and Antonio's (II.i.63-4):

Gon.   My lord Sebastian,
           The truth you speak doth lack some gentleness,
           And time to speak it in: you rub the sore,
           When you should bring the plaster.

                                            (II.i.131-4)

It is no accident that Gonzalo speaks in images of healing and that he advocates tact and gentleness. What is gentleness, but feminine awareness? It is a finely-tuned, delicately-sensitive relationship to the healing currents which flow through Nature. The healing of feeling is the feeling of healing. It knows what to do when someone is hurt. And this is one aspect of the feminine — the nurse, she who cares for the life-principle.

Sebastian will have none of this. He coldly wants the King to face the facts. He wants no evasion about who was responsible for instigating this journey. The King's son has perished and that's that.

James Hillman connects this attitude to Apollo and the ideal of the Apollonian ego in our society. The "analytical stance" of Apollo is that "which kills at a distance" or "the distance which kills". He contrasts this with the Dionysian stance which is an approach to life, "bisexual from the beginning", which "would not separate the bisexuality in the symptom, not attempt to get consciousness out of the suffering, extract the active male light from the passive suffering, since this would be to divide the bisexual totality and to favour the male knower at the expense of the female known."[8]

Fusing the consciousness with suffering, bringing the world into lived experience, is the contribution of the bisexual approach. Gonzalo is always just on the verge of accomplishing this. He, at least, allows himself to be aware of suffering.

Gonzalo's character is hidden. It only slowly emerges through the course

of the play. We shall see later the meaning of his hidden connection with
Prospero. Our approach demands a re-evaluation of his character. In the
light of this re-evaluation we see why many scholars have taken him for
a doddering, old fuddy-duddy or ignored his true value. They have not
heard the other voice with which Gonzalo speaks. He has, in many ways,
the brilliantly caring mind of Shakespeare's fool, though he wears the guise
of Polonius. In reality he is very similar to Lear's impeccably loyal Kent.
All through the play he never wavers in his noble conception of royalty.
He seems to know more about it than any of the others and yet he is usually
treated like a numbskull. He is never given much importance. This approach
is like blocking out the sound of the first violin in a string quartet. The
presence of Gonzalo is essential.

In Jungian terms the first scene of the second act explores the archetype
of Saturn, the senex. Ariel told us (in I.ii.398ff) about the renewal of the
Old King, through his strange sea-change. In the play this theme runs parallel
with the theme of the *Hieros Gamos* or sacred marriage, which culminates
in the purest expression of wholeness Shakespeare could make and still
remain a playwright, creating words and action on the stage.

Alonso is the King of Naples. He it is who stood behind Antonio's plan
to get rid of Prospero, receiving, no doubt, tribute (as Prospero suggests
in I.ii.124) for backing the heartless action. However, he has just given
away his daughter in a dubious marriage and lost (he thinks) his son at sea
and is now shipwrecked, dumb with grief. He clearly manifests the negative
senex symptoms of stony melancholy, depression and leaden weariness.
That his character sets the tone of this whole scene is clear from Gonzalo's
words to him: "It is foul weather in us all, good sir,/ When you are cloudy."
(II.i.137-8)

As a positive senex figure Gonzalo provides a balance to these negative
qualities. However, both he and Alonso are psychically related in that they
divide between them a figure whose original unity they now share. Another
name for that prime archetype of duality is Saturn. Saturn is bi-polar. As
Hillman says: "Saturn is image for both positive and negative archetype.".[9]

Within and behind Gonzalo's famous 'Commonwealth Speech' one can
hear the voice of that magnaminous Saturn who rules the Golden Age on
that magic island far away:

> Gon.   Had I plantation of this isle, my lord,-
>
> Ant.   He'd sow't with nettle-seed.
>
> Seb.   Or docks, or mallows.
>
> Gon.   And were the King on't, what would I do?

Seb.   'Scape being drunk for want of wine.

Gon.   I' th' commonwealth I would by contraries
             Execute all things; for no kind of traffic
             Would I admit; no name of magistrate;
             Letters should not be known; riches, poverty,
             Bourn, bound of land, tilth, vineyard, none;
             No use of metal, corn, or wine, or oil;
             No occupation; all men idle, all,
             And women too, but innocent and pure:
             No sovereignty;-

Seb.   Yet he would be King on 't.

Ant.   The latter end of his commonwealth forgets the beginning.
                                                        (II.i.139-154)

It is typical of Sebastian and Antonio to entangle themselves in a logical inconsistency and miss the central meaning. This is how they evade hearing what is being communicated. Notice that when Gonzalo says, "No sovereignty;-" that this is immediately preceded by the line, "And women too, but innocent and pure". What Gonzalo is expressing is the Saturnian ideal of The Golden Age, where everything returns to its pristine state, where the heavy-handed left-brain logos is transcended and the lion lays down with the lamb, where there is no exclusively male sovereignty, no petrified old king on his throne gripping the life-force of his kingdom in his iron claws of deadening power-lust. It is a dream of harmony between opposites.

In order to achieve such a goal Gonzalo sees that he would first have to do away with all rules and instruments of the dominant power-structure, executing all things "by contraries". To us today it sounds like an impossible situation, and for that reason we might refuse to envisage what Gonzalo is saying. Most people in the highly organized metropolis of modern life have little or no experience of nature uninterfered-with by men. This process has greatly accelerated since the time of Shakespeare, but the state Gonzalo is describing is still valid — it may be an impossibility in practice, but it is still a psychic reality, and it is this to which Gonzalo is referring. In constellating the archetype of Paradise or the Original Garden, Gonzalo is referring us to our original nature or the 'true mind' as the buddhists call it. And the image of this original mind in Western psyche is often depicted by mystics and referred to in Creation myths as a wondrous garden. It was painted as such by Hieronymous Bosch — The Garden of Delights: proliferating forms of a naked Adam and Eve inside seed-pods and bubbles, hiding behind transparent membranes, peering from clam-shells, surprised in an argument in mid-stream, astride pigs, griffon-headed lions and horses,

standing on their heads, embracing giant fish or owls, eating cherries as
large as oranges and strawberries the size of buffalo heads. And all the while
observed by an uncanny conference of elephant-sized birds.

It is an undisputed observation that Shakespeare lifted this speech of
Gonzalo's from John Florio's translation of Montaigne's essay *On the
Canibales*. However, it would be a mistake to stop there and not to see the
speech as a further expression of Gonzalo's character.

In times past one form of the de-structuring of Order was known as the
Saturnalia.

> The Saturnalia provided a destruction of hierarchy, law, order, and
> time. It brought back the Golden Age. All borders down, lust released,
> denials and cautions to the wind — within the limits of the 'game'. The
> Saturnalia re-incorporated the puer, his dream of freedom and his world
> outside time. But the Saturnalia, too, is an interior phenomenon, in
> that we can see through civilization and *ourselves* with the same
> Saturnalian vision. When I see myself as the caricature that I also am,
> the Saturnalia has begun, and the appearance of my craziness begins
> to shine through the system I had built against it. [10]

Gon.	All things in common Nature should produce
	Without sweat or endeavour: treason, felony,
	Sword, pike, knife, gun or need of any engine,
	Would I not have; but Nature should bring forth,
	Of its own kind, all foison, all abundance,
	To feed my innocent people.
Seb.	No marrying 'mong his subjects?
Ant.	None, man; all idle; whores and knaves.
Gon.	I would with such perfection govern, sir,
	T' excel the Golden Age.
Seb.	'Save his Majesty!
Ant.	Long live Gonzalo!

(II.i.155-164)

And, what is more, Gonzalo *does* see through himself with the same
Saturnalian vision.

Gon.	And, — do you mark me, sir?
Alon.	Prithee, no more: thou dost talk nothing to me.

19.

Gon.   I do well believe your highness; and did it to minister occasion
        to these gentlemen, who are of such sensible and nimble lungs
        that they always use to laugh at nothing.

Ant.   'Twas you we laughed at.

Gon.   Who in this kind of merry fooling am nothing to you: so you
        may continue, and laugh at nothing still.

Ant.   What a blow was there given!

Seb.   You are gentlemen of brave mettle; you would lift the moon
        out of her sphere, if she would continue in it five weeks without
        changing.

        Enter Ariel *(invisible) playing solemn music.*

                                                        (II.i.165-179)

By invoking the moon, and contrasting Antonio's and Sebastian's fantasy
of rational control with its numinous feminine nature, Gonzalo subtly reveals
the deadliness of these two "gentlemen". They are inflated, filled with the
heady fumes of hubris. They would not even hesitate to interfere with Nature
herself if they could. They respect nothing except their own wilful egoic
power-drives. How different is Gonzalo's relaxed, yet awake, benevolent
mind!

What is the real difference between Gonzalo and the three others? It is
that Gonzalo reflects a unity of what Jung referred to as the senex and puer
archetypes. Hillman says,

> We might easily believe that the difference between the negative and
> positive senex is mainly a matter of the difference between the Old King
> of power and extraversion as a profane end-stage of the Puer-Hero, and
> the Old Wise Man of knowledge and introversion as the sacred end-
> stage of the Puer-Messiah. But this simplification will not hold because
> we are involved with an archetypal structure that is not only dual as
> is the image of Kronos-Saturn, and which duality is reflected by the
> universal duality of the senex dominants Chief and Medicine Man.
> (These figures stand for the inner polarity of the senex, the two ways
> of order and meaning, neither of which is positive or negative *per se.*)
> The simplification will not hold because *the duality of the senex rests upon
> an even more basic archetypal polarity, that of the senex-puer archetype.*
> Thus, the crucial psychological problem expressed by the terms 'negative
> senex' and 'positive senex', ogre and Old Wise Man, which concerns
> our individual lives and 'how to be', which is reflected in the symptoms
> of the ageing millennium, and which influences the nature of our effects
> upon today's historical transition — this crucial psychological problem
> arises from a fundamental split between senex and puer within the same

archetype. Negative senex attitudes and behaviour result from this split archetype, while positive senex attitudes and behaviour reflect its unity; so that the term 'positive senex' or old wise man refers merely to a transformed continuation of the puer . . . *the difference between* the negative and positive senex qualities reflects the split or connection within the senex-puer archetype.[11]

In *The Tempest*, Alonso reflects the split, Gonzalo the connection, with the senex-puer archetype. Hillman defines the concept of puer eternus as *that archetypal dominant which personifies or is in special relation with the transcendental spiritual powers of the collective unconscious.*[12] Further, puer figures can be regarded as avatars of the self's spiritual aspect, and puer impulses as messages from the spirit or as calls to the spirit.[13]

Thus, Gonzalo emerges as more of a whole person than we had first imagined. Not only is he in closer contact with the feminine principle than his companions, but he also has a happy relationship with the puer, and thus with the spirit (the transcendental powers of the collective unconscious).

It is at this precise point in the play that Shakespeare re-introduces Ariel, that quicksilver messenger of the spirit, the Mercurius figure we have associated with the alchemists and with Jung's transcendent function — the puer eternus *par excellence*. In his aspect as *Hermes Chthonius*, Ariel enters invisibly *playing solemn music*. Within a few seconds everyone has fallen asleep — except Alonso, Sebastian and Antonio (those furthest removed from Hermes, the Underworld and the Unconscious). After a few words, Alonso also sinks down into heavy sleep. Before we examine the meaning of this peculiar 'sleep' and the action of the remainder of the scene, we should not miss Sebastian's reply to Gonzalo when the old counsellor chides him about lifting the moon from her sphere. Sebastian says, "We would so, and then go a bat-fowling."

'Bat-fowling' refers to the practice of hunting birds with a lantern and clubs (bats). The birds fly at the light and are brutally struck down. Sebastian means that he would use the moon as lantern with which to attract the birds. By associating Sebastian with this savage sport, Shakespeare tells us more about him in one line than an entire psychological report could accomplish. The utter absence of the feeling function is apparent even if we take the secondary meaning of 'bat-fowling' — which is 'gulling a simpleton' (OED).

2. A Sleepy Language

**20. The wolf devoured the king & after the wolf had been burnt,
it returned the king to life.**

A soporific gloom seems to descend on the play at this point![14] Suddenly,
no one can keep awake, except Sebastian and Antonio. And their 'awakeness'
is more somnambulistic than anything else. The action is eerily super-real
and mesmeric.

> *Ant.* My strong imagination sees a crown
> Dropping upon thy head.
>
> *Seb.* What, art thou waking?
>
> *Ant.* Do you not hear me speak?
>
> *Seb.* I do; and surely
> It is a sleepy language. What is it thou didst say?
> This is a strange repose to be asleep
> With eyes wide open; standing, speaking, moving,
> And yet so fast asleep.

We are indeed watching a dream. It could easily be a dream of Prospero's.
A lucid dream. A dream wherein the magician observes the archetypal
activity of the Shadow. In this dream Ariel/Mercurius embodies the
transcendent function as that pure and lucid awareness which remains awake
within the dream. Just as Hermes Psychopompus leads souls down the dread

passageways into the Underworld, Ariel leads us as spectators down in the shadow world of the unconscious.

The association 'underworld = unconscious' is further emphasized by the resonances between this scene and the underworld scene in Virgil's *Aeneid*. I feel that Colin Still is quite right to see a "pronounced resemblance between the circumstances in which Aeneas made his Descent into Hell and the circumstances in which the Court Party come to be on the island".[15] Aeneas in the Sixth Book of Virgil's epic poem arrives in Cumae from Carthage. Cumae was a harbour near Naples. His descent into the underworld is the central event in his journey from Carthage to Cumae. The 'underworld scene' in Act II, scene I of *The Tempest* is also the central event in the Court Party's journey from Tunis to Naples. We recall that Gonzalo even says that Carthage and Tunis are the same.

I would also agree with Still's understanding of the events of Aeneas' journey to the underworld as an account of an initiation. However, one would hardly think to call the events enacted in the scene before us 'an initiation'. 'A murder plot' is more appropriate. We are shown the naked face of the lust for power expressing an undisguised death-wish. These villains certainly belong to that which we "do not love to look on". Freud and Adler told us that these are typical denizens of the unconscious. Jung did not disagree; he merely added the understanding of further dimensions by saying that these creatures are not the sole inhabitants there and that they are not always the dominant ones. The unconscious, from this point of view, is not just a refuse-bin for rejected and un-assimilable contents of the ego-realm. Nonetheless, the unconscious refuse-bin fantasy does find images with which to feed itself. The walking tautological shadow of the killer-ego haunts the fantasies of the Apollian psychoanalyst.

Of course, we must look on them. As Prospero must. And see them for what they are: baldly deceptive, scheming, treacherous and ruthless.

Ant.	. . . O that you bore The mind that I do! what a sleep were this For your advancement! Do you understand me?
Seb.	Methinks I do.
Ant.	And how does your content Tender your own good fortune?
Seb.	I remember You did supplant your brother Prospero.

Ant.   True:
          And look how well my garments sit upon me:
          Much feater than before: my brother's servants
          Were then my fellows; now they are my men.

Seb.   But for your conscience.

Ant.   Ay, sir; where lies that? if 'twere a kibe,
          'Twould put me to my slipper: but I feel not
          This deity in my bosom: twenty consciences,
          That stand 'twixt me and Milan, candied be they,
          And melt, ere they molest! Here lies your brother,
          No better than the earth he lies upon,
          If he were that which now he's like, that's dead;
          Whom I, with this obedient steel, three inches of it,
          Can lay to bed for ever; whiles you, doing thus,
          To the perpetual wink for aye might put
          This ancient morsel, this Sir Prudence, who
          Should not upbraid our course. For all the rest,
          They'll take suggestion as a cat laps milk;
          They'll tell the clock to any business that
          We say befits the hour.

Seb.   Thy case, dear friend,
          Shall be my precedent; as thou got'st Milan,
          I'll come by Naples. Draw thy sword: one stroke
          Shall free thee from the tribute which thou payest;
          And I the King shall love thee.

`Ant.*   Draw together;
          And when I rear my hand, do you the like,
          To fall it on Gonzalo.

Seb.   O, but one word. (*They talk apart.*)
                                             (II.i.261-292)

    This is a chilling scene. What emerges about the character of Antonio
is that he has no moral hesitation about killing, no reverence for life at all.
Feeling does not touch him. Reason rules, completely severed from the heart.
He does not feel any conscience ("Ay, sir; where lies that?"). In fact, he
says right out: "I feel not/ This deity in my bosom". A powerful statement.
A psyche de-mythologized, desacralized, empty of any recognition of the
vast realms outside the tiny sphere of egoic will. A psyche paralyzed by will-
power, ambition and self-cherishing. *What deity* is Antonio not feeling? It
is soul.
    And just at this crucial juncture, Ariel re-enters, invisible, with music
and song:

Ari.   My master through his Art forsees the danger
           That you, his friend, are in; and sends me forth, —
           For else his project dies, — to keep them living.

           Sings in Gonzalo's ear.

           While you here do snoring lie,
           Open-ey'd conspiracy
               His time doth take.
           If of life you keep a care,
           Shake off slumber, and beware:
               Awake, Awake!

                                              (II.i.291-300)

Gonzalo wakes just as Antonio is hissing at Sebastian to be "sudden",
looks around, sees the men with drawn swords and cries out, "Now, good
angels/ Preserve the King!", and the others awake. Alonso's first words
are the epitome of shocked awakening:

Alon.   Why, how now? ho; awake? — Why are you drawn?
           Wherefore this ghastly looking?

                                              (II.i.302-3)

The explanation offered by the would-be murderers for their odd
behaviour is that they heard "a hollow burst of bellowing/ Like bulls, or
rather lions". It was "a din to fright a monster's ear,/ To make an
earthquake! sure, it was the roar/ Of a whole herd of lions." (II.i.305ff)

Gonzalo confirms the fact that there was a noise, but it seemed to him
more like a strange humming. We wonder just how much Gonzalo secretly
knows of the actual situation. When Alonso suggests that they make further
search for his son and Gonzalo says, "Heavens keep him from these beasts!",
it seems more than likely that he is referring to Antonio and Sebastian.

3. Poor Monster, Abominable Monster

21. The wolf, coming from the East, & the Dog, coming from the West, have bitten each other.

Caliban is undoubtedly the most extraordinary character Shakespeare ever created. There is nothing like him in any of his other plays or in any of the literature of the time. As figures of vitality even Falstaff and Oberon pale beside Caliban. He seems to embody the very life-force itself — sheer drive, raw energy. Yet in the Dramatis Personae he is described as a "salvage, deformed slave", and no clear image of him emerges from the play. This vagueness of form may be the deformation he represents.

Equally certain must be the connection between his appearance on the stage of the London theatre in the early seventeenth century and the appearance of the 'primitive man' on the stage of history. Explorers and colonizers had brought back reports of the natives of the New World, of the savages who painted themselves, went around half-naked and were fierce as animals. This savage was of great interest to the civilized public of Shakespeare's time — because life in the Western world had already begun to lose touch with natural man. As Trinculo says when he first sets eyes on Caliban:

> *Trin.* . . . A strange
> fish! Were I in England now, as once I was, and
> had but this fish painted, not a holiday fool there

but would give a piece of silver: there would this
monster make a man; any strange beast there
makes a man: when they will not give a doit to
relieve a lame beggar, they will lay out ten to see a
dead Indian.

(II.ii.27-34)

We remember that Prospero earlier described Caliban as a "freckled whelp hag-born — not honour'd with/ a human shape" (I.ii.282-3). In the second scene of Act II, Trinculo cannot at first decide whether this creature is a man or a fish — "Legg'd like a man! and his fins like/ arms! Warm o' my troth! I do now let loose my/ opinion, hold it no longer: this is no fish, but an islander that hath lately suffered by a thunderbolt." The phrase 'moon-calf' is used about him three times. The Oxford English Dictionary gives the following: 'moon-calf' — 1565. 1. An abortive, shapeless fleshy mass in the womb; a false conception (regarded as produced by the moon). b. A mis-shapen birth. 1610 c. A congenital idiot; a born fool. — 1620. 2. A mooning, absent-minded person — 1613.

The most used epithet for Caliban, however, is *monster*. He is called, "a very shallow monster", "a very weak monster", "a most poor credulous monster", "a most perfidious and drunken monster", "a puppy-headed monster", "a most scurvy monster", "a poor monster", "an abominable monster", "a howling monster" and "a brave monster".

Under the hilarity of the crazy comedy of Act II, scene 2, lies tragedy. It is an archetypal tragedy enacted time and time again in every corner of the globe, wherever civilization meets 'natural man'. It is the history of the North America Indian tribes and the pioneers, the South American Indians and the conquistadors, the South African tribes and the European settlers, the Saharan Touareg and the French colonialists, the Australian aborigines and the European immigrants. In every case, the so-called civilized man has acted in ways *more* savage than the savages. This is not to say that the native in each case has been pure and all-good, but there is a sense in which civilized man has outstripped the barbarians in barbarity, by using vastly superior weapons and more sophisticated methods of deceit and corruption. It is well-known, for instance, how entrepreneurs in the Amazonian basin have killed off large communities of Indians by giving them blankets infected with contagious diseases. With little or no immunity to such diseases, the Indians are very susceptible and whole populations are wiped out in the course of an epidemic. One of the favourite devices used by North American settlers was, of course, the introduction of 'fire-water' into the tribal scene.

This civilized duplicity is what we are watching unfold in the second scene

of Act II. After a few swigs from Stefano's bottle, Caliban is prepared to
bow down to him as his god. Stefano, of course, does nothing to discourage
this.

Cal.   (*Aside*) These be fine things, an if they be not sprites,
          That's a brave god, and bears celestial liquor:
          I will kneel to him.

                                        (II.ii.117-20)

★

          I'll swear, upon that bottle, to be thy true subject;
          for the liquor is not earthly.

                                        (II.ii.126-7)

★

          I'll show thee every fertile inch o' th' island; and
          I will kiss thy foot: I prithee, be my god.

                                        (II.ii.148-9)

Of course, Caliban is suffering deeply because of his rejection by Prospero,
with whom he must have originally fallen helplessly in love. Now, befuddled
by 'inferior spirits' and the supercilious recognition offered by the drunken
butler and his jester side-kick, he childishly believes that these false gods
will be his liberation.

Cal.   I'll show thee the best springs; I'll pluck thee berries;
          I'll fish for thee, and get thee wood enough.
          A plague upon the tyrant that I serve!
          I'll bear him no more sticks, but follow thee,
          Thou wondrous man.

          ★

          I prithee, let me bring thee where crabs grow;
          And I with my long nails will dig thee pig-nuts;
          Show thee a jay's nest, and instruct thee how
          To snare the nimble marmoset; I'll bring thee
          To clustering filberts, and sometimes I'll get thee
          Young scamels from the rock. Wilt thou go with me?

                                        (II.ii.160-172)

What an exquisite expression of the sensation type's apprehension of
reality! This is Caliban in his element: knowing just where crabs hide, where
jays nest, where springs can be found and where berries and pig-nuts grow.
Knowledge of the arts of survival. Instinctual intelligence. The perennial
experience of the man living close to Nature. How close this kind of

perception is to animal instinct is demonstrated by the reply given by an old Eskimo when asked "Who, at the end, knows more about the land — an old man or an old wolf?". The Eskimo replied:

> Amaguk (wolf) is like Nunamiut (man). He doesn't hunt when the weather is bad. He likes to play. He works hard to get food for his family. His hair starts to get white when he is old. Young wolves, just like Nunamiut, run around in shallow melt ponds scaring the ducks. And Amaguk is tough, living at fifty below zero, through blizzards, for months without caribou. Like Nunamiut. Maybe tougher. And Amaguk is smart. He sets up ambushes for caribou. He sleeps high up on the ridges when there are humans around. He brings his pups to a kill but won't let them stay there alone. Grizzly bears. Young wolves do a lot of foolish things. Get killed.
>
> Amaguk used to kill Nunamiut sometimes. Now Nunamiut can reach out and kill Amaguk from a distance with a rifle. Now Amaguk leaves Nunamiut alone.
>
> Times change.
>
> Amaguk and Nunamiut like caribou meat, know the good places for caribou hunting. Where ground squirrels are good. Where to get raspberries. A good place for getting away from mosquitoes. Where lupine blooms first in May. Where that big rock is that looks like acklack, the grizzly bear. Where the creeks are still running in August . . . After a pause the old man looks up and says, 'The same.'[16]

It is understandable that for generations early productions of *The Tempest* had Caliban dressed in a large, shaggy bearskin. He is a vital link with the animal realm, even when, through Prospero's disciplinary spells, he stumbles over hedgehogs, is bitten by apes and is sometimes "All wound with adders, who with cloven tongues/ Do hiss" him "into madness". (II.ii.13-14)

Caliban is actually a kind of demi-god of the forests. Although he doesn't possess magical powers of transformation, intuition and enchantment, he resembles, at least in one respect, the archetypal Celtic wizard — shaman, Merlin, in his manifestation as 'The Ward of the Wood'. It may be that Caliban and Prospero represent two sides of the wizard archetype, as they do superior sensation/inferior intuition and superior intuition/inferior sensation. Here is an account of Merlin's transformation into the Ward of the Wood from an old French text:

> It came to his (Merlin's) mind to go and divert himself in the forest of Broceliande and to do something for which he should be spoken of forever. So on the day when the three messengers departed from Calogrenant, he transformed himself into such a shape as no man ever saw or heard of before. He became a herdsman, a great club in his hand,

clad in a great hide, the fur of which was longer than the breadth of
the largest hand known, and it was neither black nor white but smoked
and browned and seemed to be a wolf skin. He took his place in a great
clearing on the border of a ditch, right over the bank, leaning on an
old mossy oak, and held his club down to the bottom of the ditch and
bent over it. He was large, bent, black, lean, hairy, old with great age,
shod without in marvellous leggings that reached to his girdle. He was
transformed so that his ears hung down to his waist, wide as a winnowing
fan. He had eyes in his head, large and black, and a head as big as a
buffalo's, and hair so long that it brushed his girdle, all bristly, stiff,
and black as ink. His mouth was as large and wide as a dragon's, and
gaped up to his ears; his teeth were white; and his thick lips were always
open so that the teeth showed all around. He had a hump behind on
his spine, as big as a mortar. His two feet were where the heels ought
to be in an earthly man, and the palms of the hands where the backs
should be. He was so hideous and ugly to see that no man living would
not be seized with great dread, unless he were brave and valiant.[17]

This gigantic, looming *daimon* seems to have loaned at least a little of his
mana to the figure of Caliban on the stage of Western theatre. A good director
would, I am sure, make use of this powerful figure which haunts the forests
of the collective unconscious. It is true that Caliban is subservient to Prospero
— but only just — and as Prospero's stature grows, the stronger Caliban
appears. A weak Caliban means a weak Prospero. The two are indissolubly
interdependent.

One thing more — we spoke earlier on about the inferior function in
relation to Prospero — how he had neglected its development and sub-
sequently had to suffer. In Prospero's case it is *sensation* which is the inferior
function, the polar opposite to intuition. With Caliban the situation is exactly
reversed: his weak function is intuition. At the end of the second Act, Caliban,
hypnotised by drink and empty promises, sings a wildly manic song of
freedom — but we know that he has exchanged a true master for a drunken
charlatan. He has totally misjudged Stefano and Trinculo, as the result of
inferior intuition. Thus, the pathos in his ecstatic song:

> *Cal.*   No more dams I'll make for fish;
>   Nor fetch in firing
>   At requiring;
>   Nor scrape trenchering, nor wash dish:
>   'Ban, 'Ban, Cacaliban.
>   Has a new master: — get a new man.
>   Freedom, high-day! high-day! freedom! freedom,
>   high-day, freedom!

                                                (II.ii.180-7)

4. For Your Sake Am I
This Patient Log-Man

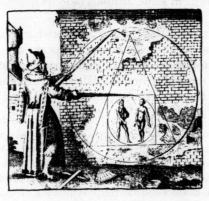

22. Make a circle out of a man & a woman, out of this a square, out
of this a triangle, make a circle & you will have the Philosopher's Stone.

If we were to approach *The Tempest* in the style of a Renaissance magus,
we would probably examine the play from the point of view as to which
planetary influences seemed predominant in each Act. I mention this only
as a useful guideline, a way of deepening the imaginative character of the
play and as a way of distinguishing its moods. And Shakespeare does play
with the moods! They change as magically as the changes in key in a musical
masterpiece. And there are also changes of key (archetypal predominance)
within the movements (acts) themselves.

This is very true of the third Act. The first scene is bathed in soft and
subtle colours. Of all the love scenes in Shakespeare's work, this is possibly
the most tender. It is the heart of the play in more ways than one. The
extraordinary vulnerability of the two young people in their growing love
for one another is almost too much to bear. It is as though we, the spectators,
had been given a new-born child to hold for a moment. Its heart is beating
and its chest is rising and falling. Breath comes and goes in its nostrils. It
all seems so tenuous and precarious — an impossibility — but there it is!
For a timeless moment our beings are suffused with the happy certainty
that love is a reality in the world.

The scene opens with Ferdinand bearing logs in front of Prospero's cell.
We recall Prospero's words at the end of Act I that "this swift business/

I must uneasy make, lest too light winning/ make the prize light''. The Prince tells us that he ''must remove/ Some thousands of these logs, and pile them up,/ Upon a sore injunction'' (III.i.9-11). Prospero, who has lumbered Ferdinand with this task, is observing him from a distance — to see how he reacts in the situation. It is just like the fairy tale in which the Prince must perform some arduous labours in order to win the hand of the Princess.

Notice the nature of the task. Log-bearing is what *Caliban* does. Prospero won't allow Ferdinand to make the same mistake as he did. The Prince must make contact with this aspect of existence in order to grow towards wholeness. In this sense, Ferdinand's labours are like an initiation. Colin Still's remarks on this subject are thought-provoking: [18]

> Let us consider the matter in the light of the supposition that the relations of Ferdinand with Prospero correspond (intentionally or otherwise) to those of the pagan initiate with the hierophant. What does this supposition imply? It implies that Ferdinand must be compelled by Prospero, as the ritual aspirant was compelled by the hierophant, to undergo certain labours and hardships symbolical of (though not necessarily identical with) those which every genuine philosopher must undergo before he can win Wisdom or Truth . . .

This is all very interesting, but surely the main point of all this — not to be obscured by higher levels of symbolic understanding — is that this scene represents *a re-evaluation of the feminine*. What is this scene about if not an appreciation, a giving of value, to the feminine?

We have seen how the unredeemed feminine principle has haunted the underworld of the Western psyche and how masculine values and virtues overruled any emergence of the feminine — as far back as the Roman era. In a talk in 1976 Laurens Van Der Post pointed out that when Troy was sacked and Aeneas could save one person, he rejected his wife and rescued his father. He carried his father on his back away from the ruined city and — ''As a result, the Roman civilisation forever afterwards has carried an old father on its back.'' [19]

During the sixteenth and early seventeenth centuries, as we have suggested, there seems to have been an attempt to lay down the old father and to lift up the feminine, though this attempt did not succeed. The many million women burnt as witches are proof of that. However, the feminine did attempt to push up — and certain visionaries and artists, like Shakespeare, gave voice to it.

In the same talk, referred to above, Van Der Post said further: [20]

A man in his deepest creative self becomes aware of the feminine element
in life. I am not talking now about feminine in the sexual, biological
sense, vit*"y important though it is. There is another kind of feminine
element in life through which a man creates: this element represents
all the caring, the feeling, the loving values of life.

Ferdinand's opening speech in Act III reveals a kind of hermetic thinking
which shows that he intuitively understands the value of his labours:

> *Fer.*   . . . some kinds of baseness
> Are nobly undergone; and most poor matters
> Point to rich ends. This my mean task
> Would be as heavy to me as odious, but
> The mistress which I serve quickens what's dead,
> And makes my labours pleasure . . .   (III.i.2-7)

Miranda, his "sweet mistress", weeps when she sees him work and says,
"such baseness/ Had never like executor". The thought of Miranda's
compassion *refreshens* Ferdinand's labours. The flowing empathy which we
met earlier in Miranda at the moment she thought the ship had been wrecked
and the men tossed into the sea ("O, I have suffered/ With those that I
saw suffer!" I.ii.5-6) is again manifested.

Miranda exemplifies soul. She is soul. Thus "all the caring, the feeling,
the loving values of life" are manifested in her. And Ferdinand is wise enough
to see how rare a phenomenon this is. By valuing soul in Miranda, Ferdinand
begins the process of soul-making in himself.

When Miranda, believing she has eluded her father, slips in to see
Ferdinand, she immediately tries to lessen his burden.

> *Mir.*   Alas now, pray you,
> Work not so hard: I would the lightning had
> Burnt up these logs that you are enjoin'd to pile!
> Pray, set it down, and rest you: when this burns,
> 'Twill weep for having wearied you.
>
> ★
>
>   . . . If you'll sit down,
> I'll bear your logs the while: pray give me that,
> I'll carry it to the pile.
>
> *Fer.*   No, precious creature;
> I had rather crack my sinews, break my back,
> Than you should such dishonour undergo
> While I sit lazy by.
>   (III.i.15ff-28)

Like Prospero, hidden in the wings, we observe these intimate exchanges from our eagle's-eyrie perspective of the spectator, far from involvement. And even so, who could possibly default Ferdinand here? The cynic in his derision merely parades his hardened heart.

Mir.   You look wearily.

Fer.   No, noble mistress: 'tis fresh morning with me
              When you are by at night.

                                                      (III.i.32-4)

Ferdinand is like a young Botticelli, painting his Venus on her shell — all wonder, admiration and astonishment. When he hears that her name is Miranda (Latin: 'wonderful woman'), he sings this spontaneous praise:

Fer.   Admir'd Miranda!
              Indeed the top of admiration! worth
              What's dearest to the world! Full many a lady
              I have ey'd with best regard, and many a time
              Th' harmony of their tongues hath into bondage
              Brought my too diligent ear: for several virtues
              Have I lik'd several women; never any
              With so full soul, but some defect in her
              Did quarrel with the noblest grace she ow'd,
              And put it to the foil: but you, O you,
              So perfect and so peerless, are created
              Of every creature's best!

                                                      (III.i.38-48)

Ferdinand believes that he has met a goddess. And who are we to say he hasn't? The ability to perceive the woman you love as a goddess is a vital step in tantric love-making, according to the hindu and buddhist yogis. Does Ferdinand realize that this is only a projection and that he is actually encountering his own anima or soul? We don't know. But we do know that this love has awakened Ferdinand's capacity for service — and service of the heart at that!

Fer.   Hear my soul speak:
              The very instant that I saw you, did
              My heart fly to your service; there resides,
              To make me slave to it; and for your sake
              Am I this patient log-man.

Mir.   Do you love me?

Fer.   O Heaven, O earth, bear witness to this sound,
           And crown what I profess with kind event,
           If I speak true! if hollowly, invert
           What best is boded me to mischief! I,
           Beyond all limit of what else i' th' world,
           Do love, prize, honour you.

Mir.   I am a fool
           To weep at what I am glad of.

                                   (III.i.63-74)

As the human girl weeps, we hear Prospero — in the wings — exclaiming his true feeling:

Pros.   Fair encounter
           Of two most rare affections! Heavens rain grace
            On that which breeds between 'em!

                                   (III.i.74-76)

Is there anywhere in the world's literature a depiction of the declaration of love to match this? Most dramatists would be more able to whistle like nightingales than to express this shy and delicate, wild and ecstatic emotion in a dialogue:

Fer.   Wherefore weep you?

Mir.   At mine unworthiness, that dare not offer
           What I desire to give; and much less take
           What I shall die to want. But this is trifling;
           And all the more it seeks to hide itself,
           The bigger bulk it shows. Hence, bashful cunning!
           And prompt me plain and holy innocence!
           I am your wife if you will marry me;
           If not, I'll die your maid: to be your fellow
           You may deny me; but I'll be your servant,
           Whether you will or no.

Fer.   My mistress, dearest;
           And I thus humble ever.

Mir.   My husband, then?

Fer.   Ay, with a heart as willing
           As bondage e'er of freedom: here's my hand.

Mir.   And mine, with my heart in 't: and now farewell
           Till half an hour hence.

                                   (III.i.76-91)

5. Under the Sign of Venus

23. **He is received into the bath, & he is born in the sky, but having become red, he strides over the waters.**

"and now farewell/ Till half an hour hence" — this is sheer ecstacy. The passion of the young lovers has set the whole stage aglow with the warmth of their being-in-love. In Alchemy the appearance of a reddening or heat in the Opus was usually taken as a sign of the Rubedo, or the stage of the reconciliation of opposites. Although this is not yet the full rich deep red of the mature Rubedo, it is definitely a change in the colour of the mood of the play. It is reminiscent of the gentle red of Homer's "rosy-fingered dawn", the first faint blush of the morning sun which heralds the coming zenith.

In *Mysterium Coniunctionis* Jung speaks of the journey through the planetary houses, beginning with Saturn and returning to Saturn, where one finds Mercurius, or Hermes Trismegistus, the fount of all wisdom. A sequence of colours coincides by and large, he says, with the sequence of the planets. It is clear that

> Grey and black correspond to Saturn and the evil world; they symbolize the beginning in darkness, in the melancholy, fear, wickedness, and wretchedness of ordinary human life . . . The darkness and blackness can be interpreted psychologically as man's confusion and lostness . . . In modern psychotherapeutic terms the analysis and interpretation of dreams confront the conscious standpoint with the statements of the

unconscious, thus widening its narrow horizon. This loosening up of cramped and rigid attitudes corresponds to the solution and separation of the elements by the *aqua permanens*, which was already present in the 'body' and is lured out by the art. The water is a soul or spirit, that is a psychic 'substance', which now in its turn is applied to the initial material. This corresponds to using the dream's meaning to clarify existing problems . . .

The situation is now gradually illuminated as is a dark night by the rising moon. The illumination comes to a certain extent from the unconscious, since it is mainly dreams that put us on the track of enlightenment. This dawning light corresponds to the Albedo, the moonlight which in the opinion of some alchemists, heralds the rising sun. The growing redness (rubedo) which now follows denotes an increase of warmth and light coming from the sun, consciousness. This corresponds to the increasing participation of consciousness, which now begins to react emotionally to the contents produced by the unconscious. At first the process of integration is a 'fiery' conflict, but gradually it leads over to the 'melting' or synthesis of opposites. The alchemists termed this the rubedo, in which the marriage of the red man and the white woman, Sol and Luna, is consummated.

. . . Astrologically, as we have said, this process corresponds to an ascent through the planets from the dark, cold, distant Saturn to the Sun . . . The ascent through the planetary spheres therefore meant something like a shedding of the characterological qualities indicated by the horoscope, a retrogressive liberation from the character imprinted by the archons . . . The journey through the planetary houses, like the crossing of the great halls in the Egyptian underworld, therefore signifies the overcoming of a psychic obstacle, or of an autonomous complex, suitably represented by a planetary god or demon. Anyone who has passed through all the spheres is free from compulsion; he has won the crown of victory and become like a god.[21]

Applying this knowledge to an alchemical interpretation of *The Tempest* leads us inevitably to regard the rapprochement of the two young lovers as symbolic of the synthesis of opposites within Prospero himself, projected onto the stage as a dramatic personification of the marriage of the 'red man and the white woman', Sol and Luna, Spirit and Soul, Logos and Eros.

In the "retrogressive liberation from the character" imprinted by the archons (Lords of the planetary houses) the individual passes through the influence of that archon and then out of its influence, "free from compulsion". In Act III, scene 1 the dominant archon is Venus (Aphrodite). Later, we will see her influence pass, but for the time being she is supreme.

Her colour is perhaps more golden than red. Homer names her the "Golden", and Hesiod does not neglect to use this epithet even when he denotes by the name of Aphrodite merely a fruitful union. Kerenyi connects Aphrodite with completeness.

> Shining in golden purity, Aphrodite, the male-female wholeness makes pale every sort of partialness. She is present when wholeness emerges from the halves and when the resolved opposites become the indissoluble goldenness of life.[22]

★

Under the sign of Aphrodite we are not dealing with something heavy and darkly earthy, with an unconscious dissolution into a state of fusion, but rather with something bright and lucid. The image of Anadyomene rising up out of the depths of the sea, is the transparent purity of complete union become visible. Through Aphrodite the whole world becomes pellucid and thus so brilliant and smiling, because in her the opposites are dissolved into unity, and this unity reveals to every living being the possibility of the same unproblematic — using the current adjective, though said in a more Greek way it would be calm sea like — situation. Following the mythologem of her birth, as Hesiod presents it, the primal unity which was broken by the bloody deed of Kronos is restored through the fact that the severed male member was received in the sea's maternal lap and there conceived the Great Goddess of love, the only one of the Titanic generation whose mother is not Gaia. Hera carries the wound of the tragic primal event, Aphrodite the healing of it.[23]

6. Thought is Free

24. The king is bathed, sitting in a steam bath, and he is freed from the black bile by Pharut.

The rational mind would like to construct theories where everything follows a fixed order, but life does not follow a programme. The alchemists knew that well and therefore gave innumerable versions of the stages involved in the Opus. Shakespeare, in *The Tempest*, is giving his own version of an alchemical process. Thus, we do not move from the Rubedo of the last scene directly into a grand finale with cosmic crescendos. The scene changes from cooing lovers to belching drunkards, from whispered intimacies to a growling murder-plot. We are back again with Caliban and his new-found gods 'from the moon', lest we should forget the Shadow side of life.

Act III of *The Tempest* comprises three scenes. Each of the three scenes discloses a nucleus of action. We know that ultimately all three centres will be brought together into one, but only when everything is ripe. This is alchemical country — where the various processes must happen in isolation until the exact moment when the ingredients can be brought together. All the hermetic conditions must first be fulfilled. And here *timing* is of the utmost importance.

We have looked at the first scene of Act III, which is centred around Ferdinand and Miranda in front of Prospero's cell. The second and third scenes deal with the other centres of action. The second with Caliban's seduction by Stefano and the drunken conspiracy to murder Prospero; the third with the Court Party and the dawning of conscience in the Old King.

The drunkenness of scene 2 is so masterfully portrayed that the real seriousness of the murder plot is often lost in the performance. It must be clear to anyone with experience of the depths of the psyche that Shakespeare is here using drunkenness to portray unconsciousness — as with the gatekeeper-scene in Macbeth, which suddenly interrupts a situation of sheer horror yet always brings roars of laughter from the audience. Words relating to water and the sea, fish and drink, permeate this scene. The three men appear to be quite awash or adrift in the sea of the unconscious. Caliban, who by this time is reeling drunk and unable to stand up, is the scapegoat, the "de-boshed fish" who has "drowned his tongue in sack". Stefano makes him crawl and grovel, even forcing him to kneel (parodying the archetypal posture of humble obeisance) in order to plead his suit: that if the three of them would only kill the tyrant Prospero, they could be Lords of the Isle. Caliban promises to lead them to Prospero asleep where — ". . . thou mayst brain him/ Having first seiz'd his books; or with a log/ Batter his skull, or paunch him with a stake,/ Or cut his wizand with thy knife." (III.ii.86-9).

Like attracts like. It is not surprising that Stefano and Trinculo stumble into Caliban. It is only strange when we begin to consider it logically. With the whole island to get lost in, how is it that these three men end up together? It only becomes plausible when we see what they symbolize in terms of the psyche. We have already seen how Caliban is almost a deified image of unconsciousness, a pure incarnation of early Prospero's inferior functions of sensation and feeling. We have seen how he is numinously conjured up by Prospero's psychic over-emphasis on intuition and thinking. At the juncture we are now concerned with, Caliban is blind drunk; his companions, likewise. It is all rather like a black shamanistic demon-possession ceremony.

Jung enjoyed using the phrase "abaissement du niveau mental" to label this critical state. This doesn't really explain anything, though the phrase is an evocative one. I am not sure whether Jung distinguished different forms of this "abaissement du niveau mental", but we know now that, though the entry into this state is fraught with dangers, it is not always and in every case equated with disaster. In fact, it does seem to be a prerequisite of the training of the shaman, who learns to enter and leave it as part of his shamanistic journey. We also know that there are different kinds and grades of shamans. When Jung refers to the loss of soul which frequently attacks primitives, he seems to be speaking of an abhorred unreal state. However, loss of soul is not only something that happens to primitives — according to the consensus reality of the popular press, it would seem to be extremely prevalent in our society.

This is a murky area. There seems to be a sense in which the shaman actually seeks the "abaissement du niveau mental", being a person who is not frightened by the ghost stories of his tribe. However, for those without the nerve of the shaman, the Other World — which is always the *real* world for the shaman — is a closed garden with a sign on the gate saying *Keep Out.* Whichever god put it there also has his minions of Repression to shut you up if you trespass into his territory. The shaman, on the other hand, has learned to walk through the walls of the garden, and he can come and go as the spirit moves him. He sees great wonders and mysteries there: secrets of life, of birth and of death. Images of shining ectoplasm writhe like dancing snakes among the words of his speech. He becomes a healer.

Maria Sabina, a contemporary Mazatec shaman, has this to say about her experience:[24]

> The more you go inside the world of Teonanacatl, the more things are seen. And you also see our past and our future, which are there together as a single thing already achieved, already happened . . . I saw horses and buried cities, the existence of which was unknown, and they are going to be brought to light. Millions of things I saw and knew. I knew and saw God: an immense clock that ticks, the spheres that go slowly around, and inside the stars, the earth, the entire universe, the day and the night, the cry and the smile, the happiness and the pain. He who knows to the end the secret of Teonanacatl can even see that infinite clockwork.

We will see later that Prospero has a good deal in common with Maria Sabina. It seems that what a good shaman possesses, and Caliban certainly lacks, is a supremely well-developed intuition combined with a strong disinclination to identify with any of the numinous powers of the unconscious.

The loss of soul can be a time of "deadly darkness".[25] In it "the conscious mind is liable to be submerged at any moment in the unconscious"; it is "the moment that latent psychoses may become acute"; and there is a "collapse and disorientation of consciousness".[26]

Jung, in this passage, is not interested in the connection between shamanistic practices and the "abaissement du niveau mental". He is interested in it as a danger accompanying a particular stage in the alchemical opus, the stage of the Nigredo, which, if successfully navigated, brings the conscious and unconscious work into harmony. The "deadly darkness" corresponds to a definite stage in the work in which terrible things can happen if the conscious is submerged by unconscious contents.

Returning to *The Tempest,* we see that this is a fair description of what is happening. Stefano, Trinculo and Caliban are involved in some kind of Saturnalia of their own (perhaps as a minor variation on the theme of the Court Party's murder-plot); at any rate, it is a revelation, however grotesque, of the true nature of these characters. All three are swamped by a flood of murder fantasies with a complete loss of any conscious standpoint from which to see themselves. They agree to kill the 'king of the island' and put their own inflated caricature in his stead.

> Ste.   Monster, I will kill this man: his daughter and I will be King
> and Queen, — save our graces! and Trinculo and thyself shall
> be viceroys.
>
> (III.ii.104-6)

Murder is very much in the air. On another part of the island Sebastian and Antonio are still smouldering with death-wishes against Alonso and Gonzalo. I have the distinct impression that Shakespeare wanted to bring these murderous impulses out of their murky caves and examine them. It should not be forgotten that this play is very strongly concerned with the recognition of the Shadow. For example, it was precisely through his own unconsciousness of the Shadow that Prospero originally lost his dukedom. If this island represents the stronghold of the autonomous complex, isolated from the mainland, and the key figures of the mainland drama have now appeared on the island, we can expect one of two things. Either all consciousness is obliterated and the Shadow triumphs, because it has not been faced — or it is recognized and finds its rightful place in the scheme of things, and the conscious work and the unconscious work come together in harmony.

Since Prospero is the central figure in this alchemical enactment of the individuation process,[27] his relationship to these manifestations of Shadow are extremely pertinent to our study.

In Act II, scene I, we saw that Prospero was intensely aware of the murder-plot against Alonso and Gonzalo. In fact, he sent Ariel to wake them just as Antonio and Sebastian were about to carry out the murder.

> Ari.   My master through his Art forsees the danger
> That you, his friend, are in; and send me forth,—
> For else his project dies, — to keep them living.
>
> (II.i.292-4)

Now a murder-plot is being hatched against Prospero himself. Is he aware of it? Yes, he is, and again Ariel is the mediator of this awareness. In fact, the comedy of this scene is caused by Prospero's "tricksy spirit", who has entered invisibly and begins to mock Caliban by announcing that he is a liar. Seeing no one else, both Caliban and Stefano assume that the words are said by Trinculo.

> Cal.   As I told thee before, I am subject to a tyrant, a sorcerer, that
> by his cunning hath cheated me of the island.

Ari.   Thou liest.

Cal.   "Thou liest", thou jesting monkey thou!
            I would my valiant master would destroy thee!
            I do not lie.

Ste.   Trinculo, if you trouble him any more in 's tale, by this hand,
            I will supplant some of your teeth.

Trin.   Why, I said nothing.

                                                    (III.ii.40-49)

A second time, when Caliban tells his cronies that he can lead them to
where Prospero is asleep so that they "mayst knock a nail into his head",
Ariel intones, "Thou liest".

To add to the confusion, a few lines later Ariel accuses Stefano of lying
(when Stefano rebukes Trinculo for accusing Caliban of lying).

Here we meet an aspect of Mercurius well-known to the alchemists. This
is the cunning and mischievous Trickster who upsets the best laid plans,
causing chaos and havoc in the laboratory, volatizing and disappearing out
of the window just when needed, scrambling the procedures, or simply self-
dividing and scattering all over the place into dozens of different symbols.
If there ever was a tricky character, Mercurius certainly is he. Ariel, and
his country cousin, Puck, are embodiments of this kind of ambiguous
psychopompic energy. One must have developed an extremely reliable
intuition in order not to be taken in by their pranks, and, even then, this
is no guarantee that one will not be bamboozled.

With Caliban, Stefano and Trinculo, however, the game is easy since
none of them has the slightest inkling of intuition. Here is intuition operating
in its inferior mode, making completely wrong interpretations of events
and mangling the nature of the possible. Ariel can lead them a merry dance,
as Mercurius often did with the immature and ambitious among the
alchemists.

At III.ii.114, Caliban implores Stefano and Trinculo to sing a "catch"
for him, and when they do, they sing a different tune than the one Caliban
remembers. Caliban says, "That's not the tune". A moment later the tune
floats through the air, played by Ariel on his tabor and pipe. This spooks
Stefano and Trinculo completely.

Ste.   What is this same?

Trin.   This is the tune of our catch, played by the picture of Nobody.

Ste.   If thou beest a man, show thyself in thy likeness:
            if thou beest a devil, take 't as thou list.

Trin.   O, forgive me my sins!

(III.ii.123-8)

Caliban has, of course, lived all his life on the island and is used to strange sounds, though he does not know their source and is helplessly under their control. His mind is as reflective as a mirror of lead.

Cal.   Art thou afeard?

Ste.   No, monster, not I.

Cal.   Be not afeard; the isle is full of noises,
Sounds and sweet airs, that give delight, and hurt not.
Sometimes a thousand twangling instruments
Will hum about mine ears; and sometimes voices,
That, if I then had wak'd after long sleep,
Will make me sleep again: and then, in dreaming,
The clouds methought would open, and show riches
Ready to drop upon me; that, when I wak'd,
I cried to dream again.

(III.ii.131-141)

This speech gives an exceptionally evocative description of the state of *participation mystique,* a kind of drifting, hypnagogic reverie where the borderline between sleep and waking is not clearly marked and the border guards have all abandoned their posts. Ariel has put a spell on them. They helplessly follow, like somnambulists following a prancing will o' the wisp through the misty marshes.

Trin.   The sound is going away; let's follow it, and after do our work.

Ste.   Lead, monster; we'll follow. I would I could see this taborer; he lays it on.

Trin.   Wilt come? I'll follow, Stefano.

Exeunt.
(III.ii.146-150)

7. The Harpy in the Labyrinth

25. The Dragon does not die, if it is not killed by its brother & sister, i.e. Sol & Luna.

On three parts of the island three separate, yet connected, scenes occur. In the final scene of Act III we witness the Court Party wearily marching towards its moment of truth. The search for the King's son has not been successful. Alonso despairs of ever finding him. It is at this point that Shakespeare introduces the image of the maze.

> *Gon.* By 'r laking, I can go no further, sir;
> My old bones ache: here's a maze trod, indeed,
> Through forth-rights and meanders! By your patience,
> I needs must rest me.
>
> (III.iii.1-4)

Shakespeare doesn't elaborate but the image is powerful enough to set the stage for the remainder of the scene. It is an image which harks back to the earliest days of our civilization: to the mysterious palace at Knossos on the archaic island home of the mother-goddess — Crete. At the heart of our civilization lies a labyrinth, a twisting and twisted, secret and dangerous mandala of paranoia. And at the centre of the labyrinth, as everyone knows, is not the Buddha or the Christ, but the Minotaur, the bull-headed man-eater.

The 'meander' is the figure of a labyrinth in linear form. It is thus a symbolic indication of the structure of the labyrinth. Now, the strange characteristic of the labyrinth or maze is that one cannot approach the centre directly; it must be done in a winding, roundabout way — the kind of path which Jung often chose to describe the course of individuation and realization of the Self.

Socrates, in the *Euthydemus* (219B) of Plato, speaks of the labyrinth as a figure whose most easily recognized feature is the indefinitely repeated meander or spiral line: "Then, it seemed like falling into a labyrinth; we thought we were at the finish, but our way bent round and we found ourselves as it were back at the beginning, and just as far as that from which we were seeking first."

Carl Kerenyi says that "Both the spiral and meander are to be taken as paths on which one involuntarily goes back to the beginning. Thus, the present-day notion of a labyrinth as a place where one can lose one's way must be set aside. It is a confusing path, hard to follow without a thread, but, provided one is not devoured at the mid-point, it leads surely, despite twists and turns, back to the beginning."[28]

At some point in time between the Minoan and the Hellenistic cultures, the labyrinth became associated with initiation. In the *Phaedo* (108A) Plato has Socrates refer to the underworld with an image characterized by many twists and turns and intersections. The experiences of those initiated into the Mysteries at Eleusis were merged in literature with a labyrinthine journey to the underworld.

Thus, the maze is a path which forces one to go back to the beginning; it is confusing; it is associated with death, initiation, and danger. Perhaps the most characteristic feature of the labyrinth is its 'perverse' relationship to the centre: "The labyrinth both creates and protects the centre, and allows entry only on the correct terms. Entry is thus initiation, a step on the path of knowledge. But before knowledge is revealed, the old preconceptions must be dissolved by re-entry into the preformal state of the womb."[29]

What about the centre? In the earliest labyrinth legends from Crete we find a terrifying man-eating monster there. So, why go into it in the first place? Either because you were looking for something quite different than a bull-headed monster or because you had to confront the monster and destroy his control over the mandala of your existence.

From a Buddhist point of view the Minotaur is an obvious symbol of Egohood, the powerful illusion that there is such a thing as an independently-existing, autonomous self or entity. The Christians have, to a large extent, ignored the Minotaur — with the sinister result of its becoming a ravenous fearsome god of the unconscious, shadowy side of life.

The Minotaur, however, is under the secret control of the Lady of the

Labyrinth, the Mother-Goddess in the guise of Queen Ariadne. She it is who knows the sacred dance of the labyrinth, the way of unwinding one's knotted conceptions of self and other in the movement towards the still centre where the man-eater is waiting. She holds the thread, the clew (ball of string) which is our clue.

Gonzalo shows his devotion to her in his opening lines — "By 'r lakin, I can go no further, sir" ('lakin means 'lady-kin'). The 'Lady' is the feminine principle — soul — which the mainland consciousness has fought so hard to suppress and destroy. Gonzalo invokes her because they are now deep inside her territory and they are, for the most part, strangers to her world. The Court Party has unknowingly reached dead centre, the heart of the maze, the dread bull's eye of Truth.

Alonso sinks into a black depression — Even here I will put off my hope, and keep it/ No longer for my flatterer: he is drown'd/ Whom thus we stray to find; and the sea mocks/ Our frustrate search on land. (III.iii.7-10) Antonio is glad to see him sinking. He and Sebastian resolve to accomplish their crime that night.

Like the deadly darkness which has enveloped Caliban and his cronies, the mood here is one of disorientation, frustration and treachery. It is another aspect of the alchemists' Nigredo, the putrefaction stage of the Work. Prospero is well-acquainted with these psychic states. His awareness of his own shadow side has given him the ability to work with the unconscious instead of against it. Shakespeare demonstrates this by bringing Prospero now on stage — as witness of the following scene.

> *Solemn and strange music; and* Prospero *on the top (invisible). Either several strange Shapes, bring in a banquet; and dance about it with gentle actions of salutations; and inviting the King & c., to eat, they depart.*

Alon. What harmony is this? My good friends, hark!

Gon. Marvellous sweet music!

Alon. Give us kind keepers, heavens! — What were these?

Seb. A living drollery. Now I will believe
That there are unicorns; that in Arabia
There is one tree, the phoenix' throne; one phoenix
At this hour reigning there.

                                                      (III.iii.18-24)

This is the Court Party's first experience of the Other World, the canny/uncanny world of the Imagination, which is Prospero's Island. The borders between what is real and what is unreal, what is waking and what is dream, have begun to grow dim and shifting. Gonzalo recognizes the creatures as belonging to the island, and he sees their essential quality.

> Gon.   For certes, these are people of the island, —
>   Who, though they are of monstrous shape, yet, note,
>   Their manners are more gentle, kind, than of
>   Our human generation you shall find
>   Many, nay, almost any.
>
> Pros.   (*Aside*) — Honest lord,
>   Thou hast said well; for some of you there present
>   Are worse than devils.
>
>   (III.iii.30-36)

Sebastian is eager to grab the food brought by the strange creatures, and when they leave, he moves in hungrily to eat. Alonso at first declines, then, encouraged by Gonzalo, agrees to partake. Just as they are about to dig in to this fantastic meal, lightning illuminates the stage, and Ariel, in a crash of thunder, appears — in the form of a harpy. As he claps his wings, the banquet vanishes.

A harpy at the heart of the labyrinth! What a surprise — no bull-headed man, but a woman-faced bird. Here we meet another of the guises of Mercurius/Ariel, the trickster, shape-shifter, androgynous conjunction of spirit and soul. Once before, Ariel appeared in feminine form: as an anima/water-nymph who enchanted Ferdinand and led him out of his despondency to where he could meet Miranda.

A harpy, however, is very different from a water-nymph. Virgil's description in the *Aeneid* is classic: "No monster is more grim that the Harpies; no stroke of divine wrath was ever more cruel, and no wickeder demon ever soared upwards from the waters of Styx. They are birds with girls' countenances, and a disgusting outflow from their bellies. Their hands have talons and their faces are always pallid with hunger."[30]

Apollodorus speaks of harpies as swift-winged daughters of the ocean-nymph Electra who snatch up criminals for punishment by the Erinnyes and live in a Cretan cave.[31] The association with Crete is startling. Robert Graves believes that the Harpies were originally personifications of the Cretan Death-goddess as a whirlwind, and he finds support for this in Homer.[32]

A Cretan Death-goddess at the heart of the maze on Prospero's island! What better image of the Court Party's mistreated feminine nature than a severe, rapacious and foul Harpy! The nobles are thus confronted by their own neglected feminine aspect — which passes judgement on them for their heartlessness and lack of soul.

Ari.   You are three men of sin, whom Destiny, —
That hath to instrument this lower world
And what is in 't, — the never-surfeited sea
Hath caus'd to belch up you; and on this island,
Where man doth not inhabit, — you 'mongst men
Being most unfit to live. I have made you mad;
And even with such-like valour men hang and drown
Their propre selves.

(Alon., Seb., etc., draw their swords)

                   You fools! I and my fellows
Are ministers of Fate: the elements,
Of whom your swords are temper'd, may as well
Wound the loud winds, or with bemock'd-at stabs
Kill the still-closing waters, as diminish
One dowle that's in my plume: my fellow-ministers
Are like invulnerable. If you could hurt,
Your swords are now too massy for your strengths,
And will not be uplifted. But remember, —
For that's my business to you, — that you three
From Milan did supplant good Prospero:
Expos'd unto the sea, which hath requit it,
Him and his innocent child: for which foul deed
The powers, delaying, not forgetting, have
Incens'd the seas and shores, yea, all the creatures,
Against your peace. Thee of thy son, Alonso,
They have bereft; and do pronounce by me
Ling'ring perdition — worse than any death
Can be at once — shall step by step attend
You and your ways; whose wraths to guard you from, —
Which here, in this most desolate isle, else falls
Upon your heads, — is nothing but heart-sorrow
And a clear life ensuing.

                                (III.iii.53-82)

Ariel vanishes in thunder; then, to soft music, the Shapes enter again and, dancing "with mocks and mows", carry out the table. Prospero, who has been invisibly observing all this, is very pleased. We hear what he is thinking, but to the King's Party he is inaudible.

Pros.   Bravely the figure of this Harpy hast thou
Perform'd, my Ariel; a grace it had devouring:
              . . . My high charms work,
And these mine enemies are all knit up
In their distractions: they are now in my power;

> And in these fits I leave them, while I visit
> Young Ferdinand, — whom they suppose is drown'd, —
> And his and mine lov'd darling.
>
> _(Exit)_
> (III.iii.83ff-93)

From this it is clear that it was Prospero who chose to confront his enemies with their guilt. The Harpy was merely carrying out orders. The King's company is now in Prospero's power, and we have the distinct impression that they are under a spell of some sort. Prospero has psychologically tied them in knots — "And in these fits I leave them."

Alonso, of all the company, has been the most affected by the Harpy's visit. He must be standing like a man who has seen a ghost at the end of Ariel's speech, for Gonzalo, who hasn't heard the words of Ariel, notices his disturbed mien.

Gon.	I' th' name of something holy, sir, why stand you In this strange stare?
Alon.	O, it is monstrous, monstrous! Methought the billows spoke, and told me of it: The winds did sing it to me; and the thunder, That deep and dreadful organ-pipe, pronounc'd The name of Prosper: it did bass my trespass. Therefor my son i' th' ooze is bedded; and I'll seek him deeper than e'er plummet sounded, And with him there lie mudded. _(Exit)_
Seb.	But one fiend at a time, I'll fight their legions o'er.
Ant.	I'll be thy second.

(Exeunt Seb. and Ant.)

Gon.	All three of them are desperate: their great guilt, Like poison given to work a great time after, Now 'gins to bite the spirits. I do beseech you, That are of suppler joints, follow them swiftly, And hinder them from what this ecstacy May now provoke them to.

(III.iii.94-109)

From what has been said so far about the situation of spirit and soul in Shakespeare's time, it may not seem remarkable that with the whole Christian tradition to choose from he barely acknowledges its existence. The Church, at any rate, was well on its way to becoming a fortress of masculine Law and Order. Shakespeare, in this scene of moral judgement, goes back to a pre-Christian religious view which has much stronger ties to the feminine consciousness. Ariel, appearing in the guise of an ancient instrument of the Furies, passes a judgement on the "three men of sin" which sounds more as if it has to do with a crime against Nature than a trespassing of human, or even divine, law. Who or what are "The powers" which "delaying, not forgetting, have/ Incens'd the seas and shores, yea, all the creatures,/ Against your peace"?

What archetypal power has been so powerfully constellated in the unconscious of Alonso that he seems to hear it speaking to him from the elements around him? "O, it is monstrous, monstrous!/ Methought the billows spoke, and told me of it;/ The winds did sing it to me; and the thunder,/ That deep and dreadful organ-pipe, pronounc'd/ The name of Prosper: it did bass my trespass.".

Most definitely, the Old King, Alonso, is suffering a sea-change into something rich and strange — an awakening of conscience and soul — even though he is perhaps the least evil of the "three men of sin".

Shakespeare is expressing a perennial truth: that beneficial actions motivated by concern for others have beneficial results for the performer of those actions and that harmful actions motivated by an angry, hateful or indifferent mind have harmful results for the performer. This universal law of virtue and non-virtue was extensively elaborated by Sakyamuni Buddha in 6th century B.C. India, and it is an epitome of the Feminine in its relationship to the life-force. The Buddha referred to it simply as *karma*, meaning 'action'. He regarded it as the natural law of the universe. Shakespeare lucidly demonstrates that mainland consciousness is quite ignorant of this universal law.

In summing up this section let us dwell for a moment on the process of integration we have been witnessing: it is clear that although Prospero has learned to know his own shadow to a great extent and has passed through the dark night of the soul, also known as the Nigredo, that he has not arrived at a place where everything just falls into place of its own accord. The final stages of integration are as fraught with difficulty and danger as the beginning ones, perhaps even more so, because the mistakes made can be that much more disastrous. The glimpses of Nigredo we are given in the scenes with Caliban, on the one hand, and the Court Party, on the other, are reminders of the many levels of the alchemical journey, the many turns on the spiral path of the Work.

Speaking of the Nigredo, Jung says that the invasion by the unconscious *can* be a positive thing — rather like the flooding of the Nile. He quotes a panegyric in the *Rosarium* on this point: [33]

O blessed Nature, blessed are thy works, for that thou makest the imperfect to be perfect through the true putrefaction, which is dark and black. Afterwards, thou makest new and multitudinous things to grow, causing with thy verdure the many colours to appear.

Notes to Part II

1. Penelope Shuttle and Peter Redgrove: *The Wise Wound*. Penguin. 1978, p. 19.
2. Colin Still: *The Timeless Theme*. p. 165.
3. *The Tempest*. Arden edition, p. 46 note 74.
4. Von Franz: *A Psychological Interpretation of the Golden Ass of Apuleius*. II.9-10.
5. Shuttle and Redgrove: *The Wise Wound*. p. 209.
6. King James VI. *Newes from Scotland*. 1591. London.
7. Wm. Perkins: *Discourse of the Damned Art of Witchcraft in Works*. 3 Vols. London 1616-18. III. p. 651.
8. James Hillman: *The Myth of Analysis*. Harper Colophon Books. Harper & Row, N.Y., London. 1972. p. 263.
9. J. Hillman et. al.: *Puer Papers*. Spring Publ., Dallas, 1979. p. 16.
10. J. Hillman: *The Negative Senex and a Renaissance Solution. Spring*. 1976. Spring Publ., Dallas. p. 84.
11. *Puer Papers*. p. 22.
12. Ibid. p. 23.
13. Ibid. p. 23-4.
14. "A soporific gloom" — see Part II. Note 15.
15. C. Still: *The Timeless Theme*. p. 145.
16. Barry H. Lopez: *Of Wolves and Men*. J. M. Dent & Sons, London, 1978. p. 87-8.
17. As quoted in Heinrich Zimmer: *The King and the Corpse*. Bollingen, Washington D.C., 1948.
18. *The Timeless Theme*. p. 182.
19. Laurens Van Der Post: *Religion and the Renewal of Man and His Societies*. Westminster Pastoral Foundation. Printed Lecture 3. London 1979.
20. Ibid.
21. C. G. Jung: CW 14. p. 229-30.

22. Carl Kerenyi: *Goddesses of Sun and Moon*. Spring Publ., Dallas, 1979, p. 59.
23. Ibid. p. 58.
24. Joan Halifax: *Shamanic Voices*. Penguin Books, London, 1980, p. 134-5.
25. C. G. Jung: CW 16. p. 268.
26. Ibid.
27. For a description of 'individuation' see index of Jung's *Collected Works*. There are many references. See, for example: CW 14. p. 471ff.
28. C. Kerenyi: *Dionysos*. Routledge & Kegan Paul, London, 1976, p. 93.
29. Jill Purce: *The Mystic Spiral*. Thames & Hudson, London, 1974, p. 110.
30. Virgil: *Aeneid*. (tr. by W. F. Jackson Knight). Penguin, 1956. Bk. 4, 204.
31. Robert Graves: *Greek Myths*. Penguin 1955. Vol. 1, p. 128.
32. Ibid. Vol. 2, p. 232.
33. C. G. Jung: CW 16, p. 271.

PART III

THE CONIUNCTIO

He ascends from earth to heaven
and descends again to earth
and receives the power of Above and Below.
His power is complete when he has
returned to earth.
— from the *Tabula Smaragdina*

1. The Chymical Marriage

27. Like the Hermaphrodite, the Rebis is born out of two mountains, of Mercury & Venus.

The *coniunctio oppositorum* in the guise of
Sol and Luna, the royal brother-sister or
mother-son pair, occupies such an important
place in alchemy that sometimes the entire
process takes the form of the *hierosgamos*
and its mystic consequences.

    C. G. Jung (CW 16.p.200)

In this book I have been tracing the vicissitudes of Prospero, a character whom I believe Shakespeare created in order not merely to defend the endangered reputation of the Renaissance magus, but to guide the would-be magus in his encounters with obstacles to full enlightenment. He did not condemn the pursuit of non-Christian, alchemical/hermetic 'pagan' science, nor was he out to damn people who wished to explore and understand the vast realms of the psyche outside the narrow confines of mainland consciousness. But he was very aware of the dangers, both within and without, in doing so. In no sense, however, was he an enemy of the Imagination. He clearly felt, like William Blake, that the Imagination is the Divine Body of Man.

    By personifying the creative imagination as Ariel, Shakespeare gave of the most precious part of himself. It was his secret, the secret of his Art, and at the same time it really is the undiscovered potential of Everyman, the paradoxical genius, creative spark or 'scintilla' which each one of us must summon to bring about his or her 'individuation'. This frail-yet-powerful, elusive, impish, daimonic, volatile, shape-shifting, delightful and terrifying hermaphroditic nymph/harpy archangel is, hopefully, what we find when we enter the laboratory of the Opus to begin our labours on the *prima materia*, the existential chaos of our lives.

The alchemists of Shakespeare's time had a secret, too. They knew that their Mercurius was not only the *prima materia*, but the *ultima materia*, the goal of the Opus as well.

In his last great work, *Mysterium Coniunctionis,* Jung wrote:[1]

> Mercurius is the prima materia. This must be dissolved at the beginning of the work, and then the dissolved bodies then transformed into 'spirits'. The transformation is effected by putrefaction, which is synonymous with the nigredo, the grave, and death. The spirits are joined together as *sponsus* and *sponsa*.
>
> . . .
>
> Since Mercurius is the soul of the gold and of the silver, the conjunction of these two must be accomplished.

Thus, it is clear that the hermaphroditic Mercurius is essential in bringing about the marriage of opposites, the 'coniunctio'.

Earlier in this study we saw that Prospero, by immersing himself in the realms of the spirit, had lost touch with soul. And, by developing his intuition and intellect, he had neglected to develop feeling and sensation. In doing this, he was in danger of becoming extremely one-sided, flying higher and higher, like Icarus, into the spiritual heavens of the Father, leaving the ground of the Mother far below and behind him. As a consequence of this, he fell from his high-flying position and, like Nebuchadnezzar, had to eat the grass of the earth-mother for twelve years, while the Imagination was imprisoned in the cloven pine of the Mother Complex.

Prospero's long exile on the island gave him the opportunity to effect the transformation of the prima materia through all the stages of the nigredo, putrefaction and death. He comes into a new relation to the feminine, to the soul, to feeling and sensation, and to the unconscious. His daughter, who has carried the values of soul and the feminine, is now grown to a young lady ready for marriage. She represents the fortunate *kairos,* or opportunity, for the exercise and development of the feeling function in Prospero's life. Then, the time arrives when Miranda needs the fulfilment of marriage. Prospero, by giving her away in marriage, will thus be in a position to interiorize what she represents. But not before he has confronted the shadows of his earlier life and mastered the treacherous, power-seeking attitudes which they represent. This is the test of his true capacity as a magus. These are the reasons why he has now brought the King's Party to the island.

Ariel is absolutely essential to all this. As Mercurius is transmuted, so Mercurius transmutes, the alchemists said. Ariel-Mercurius wings back and forth between the worlds, between conscious and unconscious, between waking and dream, light and shadow, masculine and feminine — in order to effect the final amalgamation, the conjunction of opposites: the gold and the silver, spirit and soul, Sol and Luna.

As Jung discovered: [2]

> The alchemists' endeavours to unite the opposites culminate in the 'chymical marriage', the supreme act of union in which the work reaches its consummation. After the hostility of the four elements has been overcome, there still remains the last and most formidable opposition, which the alchemist expressed very aptly as the relationship between male and female. We are inclined to think of this primarily as the power of love, of passion, which drives the two opposite poles together, forgetting that such a vehement attraction is needed only when an equally strong resistance keeps them apart.

By bringing about a union between Ferdinand and Miranda, Prospero is attempting to bring about a synthesis or marriage between two worlds, as different as Day and Night. Of course there is a "strong resistance" which "keeps them apart". We have mainly concentrated on the aspect of this resistance represented by the spirit's contempt for the soul's lowliness and its wish to fly free of soul's clinging encumbrances. There is also the aspect represented by soul's distrust of spirit's laws and numbers, its dry and cold, abstractly mathematical ecstasies. We came to the conclusion that what was wrong, not only with the quest of the Renaissance magus, but with all moth-like fascinations for the world of the spirit (or 'spirits' as the case may be), was that it neglected the return journey. One only renounces 'this world' for the 'other' one, at one's own peril. Every spiritual insight and illumination must be ploughed back into the earth if one cares at all for the quality of life lived in this world. The more one learns of the Unknown, the more responsibility one must accept for it. To shirk this responsibility only brings 'inflation' and annihilation. To quote Jung again: [3]

> It seems to me that Augustine apprehended a great truth, namely that every spiritual truth gradually turns into something material, becoming no more than a tool in the hand of man.

Shakespeare did not wish to create a tragedy in writing *The Tempest*, or he would have written a play in which Prospero is murdered in Milan or where he loses his dukedom and becomes mad, or like John Dee, dies in poverty and neglect. No, he desired compassionately to remind fellow seekers after truth of the way to wholeness, when they so easily got lost in the libraries of wisdom and the reveries of intuition. This is true regardless of any of the fantasies we project as to the 'real' meaning of the play.

Act IV of *The Tempest* is centered around the 'chymical marriage' and all the preparations for it. It opens in front of Prospero's cell with Prospero acknowledging Ferdinand's wish to be united with Miranda. Prospero hints that he may have "too austerely punish'd" Ferdinand, but that actually all the Prince's vexations "were but trials" of his love and that he was "strangely stood the test".

Prospero warns Ferdinand, however, against consummating his love before the marriage ceremony. He makes it unmistakably clear that there are greater forces involved here than in any ordinary sexual attraction.

> *Pros.* Then, as my gift, and thine own acquisition
> Worthily purchas'd, take my daughter: but
> If thou dost break her virgin-knot before
> All sanctimonious ceremonies may
> With full and holy rite be minister'd,
> No sweet aspersion shall the heavens let fall
> To make this contract grow; but barren hate,
> Sour-ey'd disdain and discord shall bestrew
> The union of your bed with weeds so loathely
> That you shall hate it both: therefore take heed,
> As Hymen's lamps shall light you.

(IV.i.13-25)

Scholars have puzzled over this speech, some taking it (and later repetitions of the same injunction) as proof of Shakespeare's strict and Puritan moral sense. It is very unlikely, however, that a man who had written some of the world's most inspired dramas of passion was under the exclusive domination of extremist moral codes. It is much more likely that what we are dealing with in this scene is the creation of the proper conditions for the coniunctio. In alchemy there were many conditions to observe — containers must be tightly sealed, temperatures must be watched unwaveringly, times must be observed for the introduction of new substances to the mixture and great care has to be taken during the whole procedure to observe the deepest respect for the influences of 'the stars'. In the famous alchemical (wordless) book, *Mutus Liber*, we see the alchemist and his soror mystica kneeling on either side of the hermetic vessel in prayer for the success of their venture. I feel that this is the internal sense behind Prospero's strict injunctions.

In keeping Ferdinand and Miranda apart sexually, Prospero ensures that the two principles undergo a purifying intensification and a further distillation. The temperature of the whole experiment increases, but so does the volatility of the substances and the danger of losing them altogether. Prospero is more nervous now than in any other part of the play. He calls for Ariel, who immediately appears, and tells him: "Go bring the rabble,/ O'er whom I give thee power, here to this place:/ Incite them to quick motion; for I must/ Bestow upon the eyes of this young couple/ Some vanity of mine Art: it is my promise,/ And they expect it from me." Although this speech seems to be referring to Caliban and his cronies, it is aimed at summoning a company of spirits whom Prospero needs in order to perform a spectacle. It is similar to a Court Masque performed at the engagement of young nobility in Shakespeare's day. Prospero wants to do something special for the young lovers — so he creates a magical pageant where the gods cross over into visible reality in order to give their blessings to the proposed conjunction.

While the three are waiting for the spectacle to commence, Prospero again warns Ferdinand to see that his passion doesn't get out of control. Venus is not allowed archetypal predominance any longer.

Pros.   Look thou be true; do not give dalliance
         Too much the rein: the strongest oaths are straw
         To th' fire in th' blood: be more abstemious,
         Or else, good night your vow!

Fer.   I warrant you, sir;
         The white cold virgin snow upon my heart
         Abates the ardour of my liver.

                                                    (IV.i.51-56)

It is in this intense and feverish atmosphere of passionate love, straining toward fulfilment, yet checking itself with the reins of Hermetic Law that Prospero's spirit-company enters to perform the Masque. The first to appear is Iris, soul of the rainbow, a messenger goddess. She calls forth Ceres (Demeter) at the behest of Juno (Hera) for "A contract of true love to celebrate;/ And some donation freely to estate/ On the blest lovers." (IV.i.84-86)

Ceres first wishes to determine whether Venus and her son, Eros, are present, because she has forsworn their company ever since they aided "dusky Dis" in carrying off her daughter to the underworld. Iris assures her that Venus was last seen "cutting the clouds towards Paphos" and that after an unsuccessful attempt to put a wanton charm on the couple, "Mars's hot minion is return'd again;/ Her waspish-headed son has broke his arrows,/

Swears he will shoot no more, but play with sparrows/ And be a boy right out.'' (IV.i.98-101). This satisfies Ceres, who accedes to give her blessings to the lovers. The two goddesses sing:

> *Juno.*   Honour, riches, marriage-blessing,
> Long continuance, and increasing,
> Hourly joys be still upon you!
> Juno sings her blessings on you.

> *Ceres.*   Earth's increase, foison plenty,
> Barns and garners never empty;
> Vines with clust'ring bunches growing;
> Plants with goodly burthen bowing;
> Spring come to you at the farthest
> In the very end of harvest!
> Scarcity and want shall shun you;
> Ceres' blessing so is on you.

Thus, Prospero, by invoking the Queen of Heaven and the Queen of Earth to bless this marriage, brings the Above and the Below into conjunction through the feminine principle. This is a vital stage of the 'project' and Ferdinand is profoundly moved by it.

> *Fer.*   This is a most majestic vision, and
> Harmonious charmingly. May I be bold
> To think these spirits?

> *Pros.*   Spirits, which by mine Art
> I have from their confines call'd to enact
> My present fancies.

> *Fer.*   Let me live here ever;
> So rare a wonder'd father and a wise
> Makes this place Paradise.

> (IV.i.118-124)

Prospero tells Ferdinand to hush ''or else our spell is marr'd'', and Iris re-appears with a group of ''temperate nymphs'' and ''sunburn'd sicklemen'' who perform a country dance. This charming interlude is abruptly broken when Prospero ''starts suddenly and speaks; after which, to a strange, hollow, and confused noise'', the spirits ''heavily vanish''. (Stage directions IV.i.138ff).

Prospero is not so entranced with his magical art that he has lost touch with the situation on the island. He has changed since the days of Milan, when he was oblivious of his brother's plans to banish him. Now his awareness is fully tuned in to the various movements on the island, though for a moment he slipped into unguarded reverie. This is why he "starts".

> Pros. (*Aside*) I had forgot that foul conspiracy
>   Of the beast Caliban and his confederates
>   Against my life: the minute of their plot
>   Is almost come. (*To the Spirits*) Well done! avoid; no more!
>   (IV.i.139-142)

2. The Ultimate Vision

28. **Two eagles meet, the one from the East, the other from the West.**

The happy celebration of the "contract of true love" is precipitously interrupted by Prospero, who has remembered that Caliban and his confederates are conspiring to take his life. Neither of the young people understands his agitation. Then, as if realizing how disturbing his behaviour must seem, he turns to Ferdinand and — for the first time — addresses him as his son, reassuring him with some of the strangest and most deeply moving words in all of English literature.

Prospero's dreamspeech has long been recognized as belonging to the greatest poetry of all time. Yet there is very little written about it. Scholars recognize its numinosity, but do not seem to know what to make of it. It is rather like a sacred stone which is worshipped in the centre of the holiest of holies. Nobody knows why it is holy, except some say that it fell from the sky.

I feel, however, that the words are a kind of meditation and that their meaning will reveal itself if one sits quietly with them and allows them to reverberate in the boundless depths of the soul.

> *Pros.* You do look, my son, in a mov'd sort,
> As if you were dismayed: be cheerful, sir.
> Our revels now are ended. These our actors,

As I foretold you, were all spirits, and
Are melted into air, into thin air:
And, like the baseless fabric of this vision,
The cloud-capp'd towers, the gorgeous palaces,
The solemn temples, the great globe itself,
Yea, all which is inherit, shall dissolve,
And, like this insubstantial pageant faded,
Leave not a rack behind. We are such stuff
As dreams are made on; and our little life
Is rounded with a sleep. Sir, I am vexed;
Bear with my weakness; my old brain is troubled:
Be not disturb'd with my infirmity:
If you be pleas'd, retire into my cell,
And there repose: a turn or two I'll walk,
To still my beating mind.

                                                        (IV.i.146-163)

What is so amazing about this speech — when it is not edited down to
its central philosophical statement — is that it is itself 'rounded' with a
poignant human frailty. Both the beginning and the end show a Prospero
who is human like us all, by no means a superman elevated above the
suffering of existence. Enclosed in this humble setting, the central insight
flashes like the fires within the brilliant Philosopher's Stone. Although the
speech seems to be about nothing, it is clearly an expression of Prospero's
deepest and most profound realization. Compare it, for example, with the
words of the Buddha in the *Diamond Sutra's* closing lines: [5]

As stars, a fault of vision, as a lamp,
A mock show, dew drops, or a bubble,
A dream, a lightning flash, or cloud,
So we should view what is conditioned.

Prospero's speech is no mere homily on the transitoriness of all things,
nor is it "the most dreary negativism that was ever put into high-sounding
words" — as Thomas Looney maintains.[6] It is a statement about the nature
of reality made by a visionary who has viewed "what is conditioned" and
seen its essential groundlessness. In the teachings of Mahayana Buddhism
this understanding is known as 'the perfection of wisdom' or *prajna-paramita*.
To this all the Buddhas are said to owe their enlightenment.

The perfection of wisdom is that which 'sees through' all phenomena
to their lack of foundation, their lack of any autonomous, independent
existence. Another way of describing it has traditionally been to call it "the
insight into the interdependence of all things". This is developed in an
individual through his awareness of voidness or *shunyata*. Not all individuals,

however, are mature enough to withstand the shock of this kind of awareness. The Sutras recount how even some of the Buddha's best disciples were known to tremble upon hearing him discourse on *shunyata*.[7]

The perfection of wisdom is thus the individual's appreciation of voidness, or — as modern translators have begun to call it — "the open dimension of being". The perfection of wisdom itself is "unutterable, incommunicable and offers no basis for apprehension".[8]

Nagarjuna (1st Century AD), the Plato of India, is generally considered to be the greatest exponent of the philosophy of the perfection of wisdom on the level of the Sutras. He championed a style of philosophy which has come to be known as the *Madhyamika*, or the 'Middle Way', because it steers a steady course between the two extremes of *eternalism* and *nihilism*. Nagarjuna considers that the perfection of wisdom is cultivated by the practice of non-clinging, or refraining-from-seizing. *To cling* is to conceive in terms of two (i.e., division). However, even the distinction between clinging and non-clinging may itself be 'clung to'. If this happens, then the comprehension of the undivided, ultimate reality is missed.

Nagarjuna approaches the problem of opposites by considering them as extremes — exclusive positions or assertions which are 'clung to'. *Shunyata* is equivalent to the Middle Way between the extremes. "For him who is in agreement with *shunyata*, everything stands in harmony; and for him who is not in agreement with *shunyata*, nothing stands in harmony."[9] When one has stopped clinging to extremes, one has reached *shunyata*. But one can also cling to *shunyata*, and this is again missing the point.

To say absolutely that something exists or does not exist is to fall into 'clinging to the extremes'. 'Is' and 'Is-not' are the two great extremes, and it is through clinging to these that the world-views of *eternalism* (that things never pass away; that the ego, self, soul or world is eternal etc.) and of *annihilationism* (that things perish absolutely or that there is no ego, self, soul, world etc.). The Middle Way is non-contention because it is non-clinging. It is non-exclusive and does not deny anything; it only rejects dogmatic, exclusive claims. "This is the sense in saying that the Buddha has no view of his own. It is precisely because he has no view of his own that he has the ability to appreciate fully the nature of every specific view, understand its need and guide it accordingly, even as he is capable of having compassion for all, able to appreciate the need of every self, every being, and extend his help to everyone precisely because he has no 'self' of his own".[10]

Shunyata is thus seen to be the characteristic of all phenomena. All things are void in essence. This, when clearly apprehended, leads not to despair, but to a sense of freedom, well-being and compassion. "For him who is in agreement with *shunyata*, everything stands in harmony; and for him who is not in agreement with *shunyata*, nothing stands in harmony.'' This simple truth is the key to the whole of the Buddha's teaching on enlightenment.

It is not strange to me in the slightest to find such a close approximation to the Buddhist concept of *shunyata* in Prospero's dreamspeech. It is the kind of statement which one would expect from a master magician. For who is the highest magician: the one who is mesmerized and ensnared by the power of his own magic or the one who sees through it all into its essential voidness?

Plato, in the *Symposium*, has Alcibiades say of Socrates that he bears a strong resemblance to those figures of Silenus in statuary shops, represented holding pipes or flutes; they are hollow inside, and when they are taken apart you see that they contain little figures of the gods. This is a very apt description of Prospero (and even more of Shakespeare). What Plato doesn't mention, but Nagarjuna does, is that if you look inside the gods, they are hollow too. The gods, the spirits, the archetypes, are just as void in essence as the ego or any other phenomenon. They are like the ''baseless fabric of this vision'' and they too shall dissolve, leaving not a ''rack'' (wisp of smoke) behind.

What is left? We are approaching the unutterable, the incommunicable. *Shunyata* is also known as the Absolute Truth, in contradistinction to the Relative Truth. On the Relative level we find all things which are conditioned, determined. What is unconditioned is *shunyata*, the Absolute Truth. Everything else, whether it be the ego, the self, the Spirit, the Soul, the archetypes or the gods, is conditioned.

Take the example of the mirror. An actual mirror is often used by Buddhist teachers in communicating the essence of the two truths and their indivisibility. The nature of the mirror itself is empty. All the world may be reflected in it, but it doesn't contain anything and neither does it cling to any reflection. Something is put in front of the mirror; it reflects it. The reflections in the mirror are likened to Relative Truth. The nature of the mirror itself is likened to the Absolute Truth.

The two truths, however, are indivisible and interdependent. The ultimate nature of the relative is *shunyata*, and one can only approach the absolute through the conditioned reality of one's existence — Relative Truth. Thus, the Relative Truth is not worse or inferior, it is simply relative. Sometimes the Buddhist teachers jokingly call it 'the false truth'. It is, however, the substantial form with which the Absolute clothes itself.

The idea of the two truths, so essential to buddhist philosophy, is almost unknown in the West. Therefore, its appearance in Shakespeare's last work is even more startling. Of course, it does not appear in the form of a doctrine. Shakespeare was a poet and a dramatist, not a philosopher. Being a poet and a dramatist, however, does not debar him from having reached an illuminated understanding. I feel that we can see traces of the realization of the two truths in Prospero's dreamspeech.

No sooner has Prospero declared the essential voidness of all phenomena than he hastens to affirm the reality of the psyche — however void it may be in the absolute sense. This is Relative Truth:

> *Pros.*   We are such stuff
> As dreams are made on; and our little life
> Is rounded with a sleep.

In saying that we are such stuff as dreams are made on, Prospero is saying that the 'stuff' of dreams is what makes life 'matter'.

As Prospero's company of spirit-actors melts into thin air, so do our lives, our projects, our loved ones, our parents and friends, our successes and failures, our memories and pains and pleasures. It is not only the cloud-capp'd towers, gorgeous palaces and solemn temples that fade like the insubstantial pageant, but even the great globe itself, the entire solar system and the distant galaxies of the universe. Where is the loved one to whom we whispered such intimacies and shared such miraculous secrets a moment ago? When the loved ones die, it is exactly as if we had just been dreaming and woken up. Thee is no way to find them again. Like a bubble, a dew drop or a flash of lightning, he or she was here, but now? Where is the sensation of delight I had a moment ago while eating a dish of strawberries? Where is the thought which I just had? Where, in fact, do thoughts come from, and where do they go? If we consider this seriously, our answer must be, "They come from nothing and return to nothing".

But we do dream, and in our dreams we are absolutely convinced that what is happening does exist. We do not remember having fallen asleep and do not know that we are dreaming. The bushmen of the Kalahari desert say, "There is a dream, dreaming us."

Images are the stuff of dreams. That is who we are. Dreamstuff. As Jung says, "Every psychic process is an image and an 'imagining' ".

In our little life which is rounded by a sleep, images arise and disappear. When they have great power over us, we may begin to speak of gods or goddesses, demons, devils, powers or archetypes. However, if we see through them, with the eye of the Imagination (and not with the blind eye of literalism), they are powerless. It is up to us whether we choose to wake up within our dreams or not. In certain forms of Tibetan dream yoga, the practitioner learns to remain self-aware while he is dreaming. In psychology this is known as the state of 'lucid dreaming'. In this state a person knows he is dreaming and has the ability to alter the scenarios of the dream as he pleases, changing an angry bull into a bubbling brook.

Up to this point in the play we have been dealing with the problem of opposites — the opposition between spirit and soul, masculine and feminine, conscious and unconscious, superior and inferior, puer and senex. We have been working with an alchemical model which attempts to unite the opposites in a conjunction. We have seen how the play moves towards this conjunction, symbolized by the "contract of true love" between Ferdinand and Miranda. We have seen how Ariel brings about this conjunction *and* how he is also the conjunction of opposites in himself as the alchemical hermaphrodite, Mercurius. We have also stressed how the union of opposites is the Opus in which Shakespeare is engaged and that it is the story of the integration of Prospero's split psyche.

In the action immediately preceeding Prospero's dreamspeech, we see spirit-actors enacting a courtly masque for the celebration of the nuptials of Ferdinand and Miranda. The *coniunctio* seems to be imminent. Suddenly, with Prospero's speech, it is as if the whole theme collapses. The dreamer comes fully awake. He looks out at the audience of his projections and shatters the spell which holds both him and them in its grip. It is as though Shakespeare had reached the border between play and reality, plunged across it and found himself face to face with the illumination of the Void. For a moment he holds the door open so that we can peer through the crack between the worlds. Then he softly shuts it, and for those who dare not admit to themselves what they have seen, he offers a way out: "Sir, I am vex'd;/ Bear with my weakness; my old brain is troubled:/ Be not disturb'd with my infirmity."

From here on, our play with opposites is forced upon a new course. Through the conjunction we begin to perceive a *coincidentia oppositorum* (coincidence of opposites). No longer a swinging pendulum between points of view, between above and below, Spirit and Soul, Heaven and Earth — but the simultaneous perception by each perspective.

For the alchemists the Opus "ends with the idea of a highly paradoxical being that defies rational analysis. The work could hardly end in any other way, since the complexio oppositorum cannot possibly lead to anything but a baffling paradox".[11] Jung subsumed all the various names for the goal of the Opus of the alchemists under one: the self. He regarded the self as the totality of the psyche. "The self is the total, timeless man and as such corresponds to the original, spherical, bisexual being who stands for the mutual integration of conscious and unconscious".[12]

The danger with identifying the goal with some *thing* is that it does give one the illusion that it exists, and we thereby become caught in the extreme of eternalism — the self as an eternal archetype, "the original, spherical, bisexual being''. What is needed among the 'Jungians', who often reify and petrify Jung's very fluid and paradoxical concepts, is the saving grace of the "perfection of wisdom" — Prospero's "baseless fabric". The Buddha often joked about his attainment of enlightenment, denying that he had 'attained' anything at all. In the *Prajna-Paramita Sutras* even Nirvana is considered to be like a magical illusion, like a dream. "For not two different things are illusion and Nirvana, are dreams and Nirvana".[13]

To make an integration of conscious and unconscious necessarily results in a "paradoxical being that defies rational analysis".

Jung summarised the multiple aspects of Mercurius as follows:[14]

1.   Mercurius consists of all conceivable opposites. He is thus quite obviously a duality, but is named a unity in spite of the fact that his innumerable inner contradictions can dramatically fly apart into an equal number of disparate and apparently independent figures.

2.   He is both material and spiritual.

3.   He is the process by which the lower and material is transformed into the higher and spiritual, and vice versa.

4.   He is the devil, a redeeming psychopomp, an evasive trickster, and God's reflection in physical nature.

5.   He is also the reflection of a mystical experience of the artifex that coincides with the *opus alchymicum*.

6.   As such, he represents on the one hand, the self and on the other the individuation process and, because of the limitless number of his names, also the collective unconscious.

3. Monster, I Do Smell All Horse-Piss

29. Three things are sufficient for mastership: White smoke, that is water, the green Lion, that is, the ore of Hermes, & stinking water.

Another turn of the spiral, another winding in the labyrinth, and Ariel appears again. This time the invisible spirit answers Prospero's question on the whereabouts of Caliban in the voice of *Mercurius Duplex*, the shifty shape-shifter (also known as *Versipellis*: 'changing his skin'), patron of duplicity, theft and trickery.

Pros.	Say again, where didst thou leave these varlets?
Ari.	I told you, sir, they were red-hot with drinking:
	So full of valour that they smote the air
	For breathing in their faces; beat the ground
	For kissing of their feet; yet always bending
	Towards their project. Then I beat my tabor;
	At which, like unback'd colts, they prick'd up their ears,
	Advanc'd their eyelids, lifted up their noses
	As they smelt music: so I charm'd their ears,
	That, calf-like, they my lowing follow'd, through
	Tooth'd briers, sharp furzes, pricking goss, and thorns,
	Which enter'd their frail shins: at last I left them
	I' th' filthy-mantled pool beyond your cell,
	There dancing up to th' chins, that the foul lake
	O'erstunk their feet.

    Pros.   This was well done, my bird.
    Thy shape invisible retain thou still:
    The trumpery in my house, go bring it hither,
    For stale to catch these thieves.

    Ari.   I go, I go. (*Exit*)
                                 (IV.i.170-186)

After leading Stefano, Trinculo and Caliban through gorse and thorn-bushes, Ariel leaves them in a stinking, filthy pool up to their chins in slime. It is an extraordinary image, reminiscent of Dante.

Mercurius Duplex is like the will-o'-the-wisp. He charms and seduces and leads one off into the treacherous bogs, dancing on ahead with his ambiguous, winking lantern or piping a captivating melody. The three drunkards are completely taken in by his enchanting music. But the commander and his spirit are not through with them yet. There is more in store. Prospero instructs Ariel to hang out some flashy clothes with which to catch them. When he is alone, Prospero muses bitterly on Caliban.

    Pros.   A devil, a born devil, on whose nature
             Nurture can never stick; on whom my pains,
             Humanely taken, all, all lost, quite lost;
             And as with age his body uglier grows,
             So his mind cankers. I will plague them all,
             Even to roaring.
                               (IV.i.188-193)

This passage has a completely different flavour to it than the dreamspeech. This is the world of relative truth, and in it, there are devils as well as gods, darkness as well as light. Prospero has learned that he cannot ignore the Shadow — he must live the contradiction of perceiving the absolute, yet living amidst the relative. This is the open and paradoxical secret. It is what Jung was referring to when he wrote:

> The man who is only wise and only holy interests me about as much as the skeleton of a rare saurian, which would not move me to tears. The insane contradiction, on the other hand, between existence beyond Maya in the cosmic Self, and that amiable human weakness which fruitfully sinks may roots into the black earth, repeating for all eternity the weaving and rending of the veil . . . — this contradiction fascinates me; for how else can one perceive the light without the shadow, hear the silence without the noise, attain wisdom without foolishness?"[15]

Ariel returns, "loaden with glistering apparel" and hangs the garments out in front of Prospero's cell. He and the magus retreat to watch the scene from an invisible perspective as Caliban, Stefano and Trinculo enter, all wet and dripping from the "foul lake".

The appearance of the three muddy men in tattered clothes and mad demeanour is not only comic — it is symbolic of the utter delusion that resides in the auto-intoxicated, selfish will-to-power which desires to overthrow true realization. Their immersion in the "filthy-mantl'd pool" has been an inverted initiation, a pseudo-baptism in the stagnant waters of their self-deceit. The experience has not given them pause — they have learned nothing from their pains. Caliban is still obsessed with the wish to murder Prospero, warning the others to "tread softly" so that even "the blind mole may not/ Hear a footfall". Stefano is outraged with Caliban and blames him for the tricks of his "harmless fairy" who has "played the Jack" (Jack o'lantern; will-o'-the-wisp) with them. Trinculo cannot stand the stink which now envelopes them all.

> *Trin.*   Monster, I do smell all horse-piss; at which my
>   nose is in great indignation.
>
> (IV.i.199-200)

They are arguing about the loss of their bottles in the pool when Trinculo notices the "glistering apparel".

> *Trin.*   O King Stefano! O peer! O worthy Stefano!
>   Look what a wardrobe here is for thee!
>
> *Cal.*   Let it alone, thou fool; it is but trash.
>
> (IV.i.222-224)

Stefano and Trinculo are immediately caught by their own projections; they are so enmeshed in the fantasies they have about themselves, that they totally ignore where they are — in front of Prospero's cave. While they set about stealing the clothes, Caliban rages at them.

> *Cal.*   I will have none on 't: we shall lose our time,
>   And all be turn'd to barnacles, or to apes
>   With foreheads villainous low.
>
> *Ste.*   Monster, lay-to your fingers: help to bear this away
>   where my hogshead of wine is, or I'll turn you out
>   of my kingdom: go to, carry this.
>
> *Trin.*   And this.
>
> *Ste.*   Ay, and this.
>
> *A noise of hunters heard. Enter divers Spirits, in shape of dogs
> and hounds, hunting them about*; Prospero *and* Ariel *setting them on.*

Pros.   Hey, Mountain, hey!

Ari.   Silver! there it goes, Silver!

Pros.   Fury, Fury! there, Tyrant, there! hark, hark!

(*Cal., Ste., and Trin. are driven out*)

Go charge my goblins that they grind their joints
With dry convulsions; shorten up their sinews
With aged cramps; and more pinch-spotted make them
Than pard or cat o' mountain.

Ari.   Hark, they roar!

Pros.   Let them be hunted soundly. At this hour
Lies at mercy all mine enemies:
Shortly shall all my labours end, and thou
Shalt have the air at freedom: for a little
Follow, and do me service.

(*Exeunt*)

                                        (IV.i.247-266)

4. Deeper Than Did Ever Plummet Sound

30. This is the dragon which devours its own tail.

Gazing into the alchemical vessel of our hermetic drama, we can now glimpse subtle shapes evolving within its vaporous interior. On the island, Ferdinand and Miranda bask in the blessings of the Queen of Heaven and the Queen of Earth. The *Hieros Gamos* is soon to be performed. Deep within the labyrinth the good and evil nobles of Milan and Naples career towards the exit. The journey through the planetary houses has come full circle. The rich, black earth of the Nigredo has been exposed. The spirit-actors have melted into thin air. Our revels now are ended and the Opus is approaching the crowning moment when all the components necessary for the *coincidentia oppositorum* will come together to create that wholeness that "puts an end to conflict", as Jung said, "or at least draws its sting"![6]

ACT V

Scene 1. — (*Before the Cell of Prospero.*)
Enter Prospero *in his magic robes, and* Ariel.

Pros.   Now does my project gather to a head:
            My charms crack not; my spirits obey; and time
            Goes upright with his carriage. How's the day?

Ari.   On the sixth hour; at which time, my lord,
    You said our work should cease.

                            (V.i.1-5)

In the Arden edition of *The Tempest*, Frank Kermode points out some extremely interesting references to alchemy in these opening lines. His notes to these lines read as follows: [17]

1. *project*: Undertaking, venture; but with a hint of the alchemical "projection", the last phase of the philosopher's experiment. "Project" could be used of the experiment as a whole. The metaphor in *gather to a head* (which is not unique) is certainly of a boil; perhaps there is some analogy between the process of a boil's development and the alchemical process. Both are slow, and the latter is also expected to discharge a new substance.
2. *crack*: Furness was certainly right in suspecting an alchemical reference. "Crack" is used of the explosion of retorts, etc., which brings Mammon's venture to disaster in Jonson's *Alchemist*, IV.v.56.

Four hours have passed since the opening scene of the storm. During this time Prospero has carefully separated and combined the elements of his "project", using the distillations and solutions of twelve long years of patient labour. *Even the stars are in their correct positions for the best result.*

Prospero asks Ariel how the King's Party is faring. Ariel replies that they are all prisoners in the grove beyond his cell. The King, Sebastian and Antonio are spellbound, and the others mourn over them, "brimfull of sorrow and dismay".

Ari.   . . . but chiefly
    Him you term'd, sir, "The good old lord, Gonzalo";
    His tears run down his beard, like winter's drops
    From eaves of reeds. Your charm so strongly works 'em,
    That if you now beheld them, your affections
    Would become tender.

Pros.   Dost thou think so, spirit?

Ari.   Mine would, sir, where I human.

Pros.   And mine shall.
    Hast thou, which art but air, a touch, a feeling
    Of their afflictions, and shall not myself,
    One of their kind, that relish all as sharply
    Passion as they, be kindlier mov'd than thou art?
    Though with their high wrongs I am struck to th' quick,
    Yet with my nobler reason 'gainst my fury

Do I take part: the rarer action is
In virtue than in vengeance: they being penitent,
The sole drift of my purpose doth extend
Not a frown further. Go release them, Ariel:
My charms I'll break, their senses I'll restore
And they shall be themselves.

(V.i.15-32)

We owe it to Dover Wilson in his wise and loving talk on "The Meaning of The Tempest"[18] for pointing out the great transformation in Prospero implied in the above lines. Even in dramatic terms where emotions and actions are greatly condensed, the transformation is extraordinarily abrupt. It is an accelerated (alchemical) reaction, and Ariel is the catalyst. Dover Wilson says, "The conversion of Prospero is sudden, like other conversions in Shakespeare: the age believed in sudden conversions. But it is none the less real on that account, and takes Prospero himself as much by surprise as it takes us. At the beginning of the scene he boasts that his 'charms crack not'; twenty lines later he is declaring, 'My charms I'll break'. What is it that causes his 'fury' thus magically, almost involuntarily, to subside like the raging sea when the tempest has ceased to vex it? There is no hint of moral compunction, no reminder, as in Portia's famous speech, of the promptings of religion. The conversion is an aesthetic one; it is made at the suggestion of Ariel, who is surely the genius of dramatic poetry; *and is brought about by the force of the imagination*, which compels Prospero to put himself in the place of his enemies, to 'passion as they'." (Italics mine.)

The force of the imagination. This is the force that leads towards reconciliation — and makes compassion possible. And, as Ariel is the personification of the Imagination (Mercurius), so is he the genius of dramatic poetry; indeed he is the archetype of genius, the genius of all archetypes.

Prospero's respect for Ariel, his being 'in-formed' by the angelic sense of the message-bearer's words and the growing sense of unity between the two — all hint at a new level of integration in the magus.

It is not the least bit strange that forgiveness is directly constellated as a conscious attitude through this integration. This outer reconciliation reflects Prospero's inner reconciliation between spirit and soul. Spirit is not always moved to forgive — it could just as easily declare a holy war (crusade, 'jihad') on its enemy, whereas the soul tends to abandon itself to what may come and silently suffer the worst atrocities. Prospero's inner *coincidentia oppositorum* has now enabled soul to stand up to spirit and claim recognition of *its* value. Soul has proved to spirit that it (spirit) is not totally autonomous and unconnected, that it simply cannot do exactly what it wills and that it needs soul in order to fulfil itself and to reflect itself in. Surely, "the rarer action is in virtue than in vengeance", but how is this noble thought ever to take root in the world if soul is invalidated as inferior, stupid, weak and second-rate?

That soul is essentially *the imaginative possibility in our natures*[19] is a perennial teaching of the esoteric schools of Western hermetical tradition — though it has always been anathema to the Church and the politics of monotheism. In contradistinction to the spirit, which aims at a pure and intellectual singularity, the soul allows an unbounded proliferation of images, a fecund and bottomless depth and a plurality of organisations of psychic perspective around the myriad archetypal nuclei. Shakespeare's dramatic work is an astounding expression of this soul tradition, hermetic and heretic at one and the same time. In *The Tempest*, as I have tried to show, Shakespeare offers us a glimpse into the secret workings of his Art. In this play all his sympathy, and ours, by force of his dramatic genius, is with the fate of a Renaissance magus, who begins by enslaving himself to the spirit and, after much suffering, learns to serve soul, until, finally, he is able to discover their equal value and mutual interdependence in his personal existence.

In the last quarter of the twentieth century we are gradually returning to an appreciation of the soul, but now no longer reified as an entity, but rather seen as a viewpoint, a reflective perspective.

Nowhere is *this* sense of soul better articulated than in the work of Jung and his successors, in particular that of James Hillman. In his major work, "Revisioning Psychology", he says:[20]

> In another attempt upon the idea of soul I suggested that the word refers to that unknown component which makes meaning possible, turns events into experiences, is communicated in love, and has a religious concern. These four qualifications I had already put forth some years ago; I had begun to use the term freely, usually interchangeably with psyche (from Greek) and anima (from Latin). Now I am adding three necessary modifications. First, "soul" refers to *deepening* of events into experiences; second, the significance soul makes possible, whether in love or in religious concern, derives from its special relation *with death*. And third, by "soul" I mean the imaginative possibility in our natures, the experiencing through reflective speculation, dream, image and *fantasy* — that mode which recognizes all realities as primarily symbolic or metaphorical.

Now, at long last we are able to approach Prospero's next speech — the famous 'abjuration of magic' soliloquy. Of the many enigmas of *The Tempest* this seems to me to be the most misunderstood.[21]

As Frank Kermode and others have pointed out, Prospero's speech is a

31.

skilful re-working of Medea's incantation in Book VII of Ovid's
Metamorphoses. Before we try to understand the full implications of this
soliloquy, we should recall the context from which it is derived. Kermode
claims that Shakespeare went to Ovid as to a *locus classicus* for his picture
of the witch.[22] I believe that there is more to it than that. Medea is more
than a sorceress and an archetypal witch. Other classical figures, like the
witch of Endor and *Potnia theron* (Mistress of the wild animals) Circe, abound
in Western literature. What characterizes Medea above all else is that she
is a murderess and a life-restorer. Her magic is not an art, like Circe's,
it is a science of life and death, a science that invokes the triple goddess of
the moon, Hecate. As Carl Kerenyi says "Hecate commands the secret
knowledge that is not Apollonic; in her the lunar displays its understanding
of the most secret exits and entries of life's origin and its termination".[23]

It is to Hecate that Medea prays in the incantation Shakespeare took
from Ovid's *Metamorphoses*. The use, however, to which Shakespeare puts
this incantational poetry is somewhat altered. Whereas Medea, in Ovid's
account, is invoking the demonic energy of Hecate and the spirits of the
night to aid her in the magical transformation of Jason's father from an
old decrepit man into a rejuvenated youth, Prospero is hailing the spirits
of nature, by whose aid he has "bedimm'd the noontide sun" and worked
many other feats *contra naturam*. *Then* he abjures the practice of this "rough
magic".

But can one abjure something in this way which one has not used and
mastered? Prospero is here telling us that he has actually been practising
witchcraft in the highest degree. And this kind of magic is not the masculine
tradition of the Renaissance magus — with all the mathematical, mystical
architectonics of Bruno, Fludd and John Dee — it is the feminine tradition
whose patron is the lunar goddess, Hecate; thus Prospero at last announces
his secret connection with Sycorax and "her mischiefs manifold and sorceries
terrible".

It is no accident that Shakespeare has Prospero echo the incantations
of Medea. Behind and inside this overt rejection of magic, there is the
intimate identification with the feminine wisdom — with all its mysterious
knowledge of the forces of life and death, the cycles and tides of Nature,
the "consciousness of the blood". In Prospero's speech there is none of
the cynicism, ridicule or aversion manifested by Ben Jonson, for example,
in his dealings with magic and alchemy. There is only great affection and
poignant clarity of observation, mixed with a certain tinge of visionary
melancholy.

Pros.   Ye elves of hills, brooks, standing lakes, and groves;
And ye that on the sands with printless foot
Do chase the ebbing Neptune, and do fly him
When he comes back; you demi-puppets that
By moonshine do the green and sour ringlets make,
Whereof the ewe not bites; and you whose pastime
Is to make midnight mushrooms, that rejoice
To hear the solemn curfew; by whose aid —
Weak masters though ye be — I have bedimm'd
The noontide sun, call'd forth the mutinous winds,
And 'twixt the green sea and the azur'd vault
Set roaring war: to the dread rattling thunder
Have I given fire, and rifted Jove's stout oak
With this own bolt; the strong-bas'd promontory
Have I made shake, and by the spurs pluck'd up
The pine and cedar: graves at my command
Have wak'd their sleepers, op'd, and let 'em forth
By my so potent Art. But this rough magic
I here abjure; and, when I have requir'd
Some heavenly music, — which even now I do, —
To work mine end upon their senses, that
This airy charm is for, I'll break my staff,
Bury it certain fathoms in the earth,
And deeper than did ever plummet sound
I'll drown my book.

My view of this is that Prospero, like the Buddhist tantric masters and Mahasiddhas of medieval India (Saraha, Shantipa, Kanapa, Ghantipa, Kukuripa etc.), rejects 'black' magic, that is, magic performed to aggrandise the ego, gain power over others and do harm. Beyond that he is also abjuring all *outer* manifestations of magic.

There is a view that tends to see Prospero as a pagan renouncing his heathen practices. In his book on the play D. G. James, for example, says that ". . . it is still true that *The Tempest* provides an ending to the history of magic and the occult in Western Europe".[24] He expands his view as follows:[25]

> I am saying that when Prospero declares he will abjure his rough magic we behold his creator, the greatest spirit of our civilization, in these early days, saying farewell to a whole region of the human imagination . . .
> . . . now, in the writings of Shakespeare, we see the farewell of the human imagination to magic and all its ways, and to the hideous figures which moved in it so long and to its inexpressible terror. Shakespeare is no doubt ahead of his age, as we should expect, and shaping its future.

There is something, in my estimation, not quite right about this. I do not believe that Shakespeare's intention in writing *The Tempest* was to make a political statement condemning magic. Nor do I believe that he was in the vanguard of any such movement. *The Tempest* is a magical play. Magic is absolutely essential to Prospero in achieving his salvation.

Shakespeare was ahead of his age, certainly. But, I feel that he was much further ahead of it than Mr James gives him credit for. I do not feel that we have yet fully understood Shakespeare's message. This study is only a beginning. Prospero breaks his staff, yes. But what else could he do, given the political climate? *The Tempest* was first performed in the banqueting hall at Whitechapel with King James as the guest of honour. James was notorious for hating and fearing anyone having any connections with the practices of witchcraft. He obviously was not in the position to appreciate the subtleties of Shakespeare's understanding of the subject. Shakespeare had a message for the far distant future, and he had to say it and get it said in such a way that it would not be destroyed.

As an imaginative possibility I would like to suggest an alternative view to that expressed by Mr James. Let us imagine that Prospero makes a great to-do about breaking his staff in the same way that the Cumaen Sybil threw drugged meat to Triple-Headed Cerberus who guards the gates of Hell. Let us suppose that Prospero breaks his staff, not in a gesture of Puritanical pique and hatred of the Imagination, but as a further magical gesture of his Art. Let us suppose that he is erasing his tracks.

Further, let us imagine that Prospero drowns his book, not as a "farewell to a whole region of the human imagination", but because he wants to put it out of reach of those who would misuse it and because he wants to return it to where it originally came from — the collective unconscious. There is will stay until it is needed again by another Prospero in the future. There is more to drowning a book than meets the eye.

5. The Magic Circle of the Rarer Action

32. **When the king had drunk from the waters, he became ill, after he had been treated by the physicians he regained his heath.**

Prospero, according to Shakespeare's stage directions, has made a circle in front of his cell. It is into this space that his enemies — to the strains of "some heavenly music" — are now drawn. They are still mesmerized, still deep in a hermetic trance.

Like any image, the circle has no absolutely fixed psychological meaning. Rather, it resembles an inviting tree at dusk, giving shelter to many meanings which come to roost like birds from different directions. Thus, what we are dealing with is a clustering of sense. The circle, as C. G. Jung has so amply demonstrated, is everywhere a symbol of wholeness — and thus a hieroglyph for the self. The magician's circle, the store circles of the ancients, the witches' circle of conjuration and the holy circle of religious dance and ritual are all ringing ripples of this archetypal circle. The circle protects, but it also contains; it excludes, yet it provides the space for integration.

The action in the play has nearly come full circle. The beginning (Prospero's expulsion from Milan) and the end (his return) are close to meeting. Also, the various fragmented, cut-off, neglected and denied aspects of his psyche are now being brought face-to-face. As Prospero has learned to accept his own cut-off aspects, he is now able to accept the persons upon whom he had previously projected these unconscious contents. This is the essential pre-requisite for all true forgiveness. By bringing his enemies *into* the circle, Prospero is confronting *himself* in them — as well as allowing them to confront him.

Dramatically, this section of the play needs very sensitive direction if the feeling aspect is to emerge undamaged. The tempo is slow and majestic. The 'unconscious' nobles give an air of timelessness to the scene, flailing about like deranged sleepwalkers in an underwater ballet. As they begin to come to their senses, a parallel development occurs in Prospero. He is almost ordinary now. His Opus is nearing its finale. He resembles those tribal shamans who, after going into ecstatic trances where they work wonders and communicate with all sorts of beings not of this world, return to their 'normal' selves, as if coming out of a divine seizure. Now, although still wearing his magic robes, he has reached the point where magic can take him no further. Here, what is needed is *heart* — a courage (Fr. 'coeur'; Gk. 'ker') born of *soul* — if a transformation is to be effected.

This is Prospero's greatest moment. All that follows will be confirmation, celebration and adornment. Nevertheless, this ''reconciliation scene'', as it has been often called, does not just *happen* in a matter-of-fact, perfunctory manner. The atmosphere is permeated with the incense of the numinous, of danger not yet passed; a feeling mode of grief and dark emotion. Let us look at the text:

> *Here enters* Ariel *before: then* Alonso, *with a frantic gesture, attended by* Gonzalo; Sebastian *and* Antonio *in like manner, attended by* Adrian *and* Francisco: *they all enter the circle which* Prospero *had made, and there stand charm'd; which* Prospero *observing, speaks:*

> *Pros.*   A solemn air, and the best comforter
>   To an unsettled fancy, cure thy brains,
>   Now useless, boil'd within thy skull! There stand,
>   For you are spell-stopp'd.
>   Holy Gonzalo, honourable man,
>   Mine eyes, ev'n sociable to the show of thine,
>   Fall fellowly drops. The charm dissolves apace;
>   And as the morning steals upon the night,

>   Melting the darkness, so their rising senses
>   Begin to chase the ignorant fumes that mantle
>   Their clearer reason. O good Gonzalo,
>   My true preserver, and a loyal sir
>   To him thou follow'st!

> (V.i.58-70)

The image, ''As the morning steals upon the night'', is a definite indication that the alchemical opus is reaching its culmination. And, as it does, Prospero allows himself to weep again — this time with compassion for Gonzalo, his "true preserver". Next, he looks at the King and the King's brother:

(*Pros.*)   Most cruelly
         Didst thou, Alonso, use me and my daughter:
         Thy brother was a furtherer in the act.
         Thou art pinch'd for't now, Sebastian.

                                             (V.i.71-74)

Last of all, he turns his gaze on his own brother. This is the most difficult
task of all:

(*Pros.*)   Flesh and blood,
         You, brother mine, that entertain'd ambition,
         Expell'd remorse and nature; whom, with Sebastian, —
         Whose inward pinches therefor are most strong, —
         Would here have kill'd your King; I do forgive thee,
         Unnatural though thou art.

                                             (V.i.74-79)

The nobles are still 'asleep', however, and Prospero has yet to confront
Antonio 'awake'. But the ice has been broken, the water is flowing again.
We know that Prospero has mastered himself and that he will not back down
from the confrontation. Seeing that the men are coming awake, he takes
off his magic robes and resumes his role as the Duke of Milan. The circle
is complete.

(*Pros.*)   Their understanding
         Begins to swell; and the approaching tide
         Will shortly fill the reasonable shore,
         That now lies foul and muddy. Not one of them
         That yet looks on me, or would know me: Ariel,
         Fetch me the hat and rapier in my cell:
         I will discase me, and myself present
         As I was sometime Milan: quickly, spirit;
         Thou shalt ere long be free.

                                             (V.i.79-87)

Of course, Ariel must soon be free! The internal consistency of these lines
is remarkable. For when the self is realised, then what need for personal
familiars? Ariel is a kind of world-soul/spirit. His true universality as *Lumen
naturae*, the light of nature, is clearly expressed in this excstatic song:

                   Where the bee sucks, there suck I:
                   In a cowslip's bell I lie;
                   There I couch when owls do cry.
                   On the bat's back I do fly

> After summer merrily.
> Merrily, merrily shall I live now
> Under the blossom that hangs on the bough.
>
> (V.i.88-94)

Ariel's lovely song is an impeccable manifestation of the perennial quicksilveriness of the imagination. It can not be pinned down! Much to the chagrin and frustration of the literalizing mind, which always wants to know where it has everything, esctatic gnosis is sometimes lying in a cowslip's bell, sometimes flying on the back of a bat, but never in the dead fragments of dissected psyche.

Don't you sense the excitement here? Suddenly, it is as if one had reached the top of a ridge, after walking ages in an overclouded, dark valley. One has come out of the clouds and into a vast panorama of snow-capped peaks shining in a clear, blue sky.

Ariel's excitement is counterpointed by Prospero's nostalgia: "Why, that's my dainty Ariel! I shall miss thee;/ But yet thou shalt have freedom: so, so, so." (V.i.95-96). Prospero instructs Ariel in his penultimate task — to go to the King's ship and bring him the master and the boatswain. Ariel exits, but not before giving us an unforgettable image for the characteristic speed of the imagination: [26]

> *Ari.*   I drink the air before me, and return
>   Or ere your pulse twice beat.
>
> (V.i.102-103)

The nest three lines, although traditionally assigned to Gonzalo in the Folio edition, seem to me to belong most definitely to Alonso. I have no support for this, other than my understanding of the play, but I feel that when heard as spoken by Alonso, they make unquestionable sense, whereas it is a highly unlikely speech for "Holy Gonzalo". Let us hear them then as if spoken by Alonso:

> *(Alon.)*   All torment, trouble, wonder and amazement
>   Inhabits here: some heavenly power guide us
>   Out of this fearful country!
>
> (V.i.104-106)

Prospero then addresses the awakening King and explains who he is, welcoming him. The King is shattered by this new revelation and begs for pardon for his wrongs.

> *Pros.*   Beyond, sir King,
>   The wronged Duke of Milan, Prospero:

> For more assurance that a living Prince
> Does now speak to thee, I embrace thy body;
> And to thee and thy company I bid
> A hearty welcome.

Alon.   Whether thou be'st he or no,
> Or some enchanted trifle to abuse me,
> As late I have been, I not know: thy pulse
> Beats, as of flesh and blood; and, since I saw thee,
> Th' affliction of my mind amends, with which,
> I fear, a madness held me: this must crave —
> And if this be at all — a most strange story.
> Thy dukedom I resign, and do entreat
> Thou pardon me my wrongs. — but how should
>   Prospero
> Be living and be here?

                                        (V.i.106-120)

Prospero, of course, is not interested in answering questions now. In deference to custom he has welcomed the King first, but it is Gonzalo he wishes most to embrace again.

Pros.   First, noble friend,
> Let me embrace thine age, whose honour cannot
> Be measur'd or confined.

                                        (V.i.120-122)

I feel now confirmed in the intuition that Shakespeare must have meant Gonzalo to have a special place in Prospero's heart. The greeting is one of deepest respect, a salutation one might expect from a now-mature pupil to his master. Any why not? Can not a counsellor be a mentor to a king? If this supposition is true, then we have discovered a new dimension in the play: the hidden, guiding influence of Gonzalo on Prospero. And, even though he may have surpassed his teacher in many ways, Prospero nonetheless accords him the highest honour in saying that his honour is too great to be measured.

By now, the rest of the company are awake. Prospero, seeing that Sebastian and Antonio have recovered their senses, turns and speaks a quiet aside to them:

(Pros.) But you, my brace of lords, were I so minded,
> I here could pluck his highness' frown upon you,
> And justify you traitors: at this time
> I will tell no tales.

Seb.   *(Aside)* The devil speaks in him.

                                        (V.i.126-129)

Such a remark that Sebastian makes was often enough to initiate a terrible imbroglio, ending in witch-trials and death by burning or hanging — in Shakespeare's day. By putting this accusation in the mouth of such a villain as Sebastian, however, Shakespeare shows its political and defamatory character. No one, at this point in the play, however unsympathetic to the magical tradition, could possibly see Prospero as possessed by the devil. And yet, how *does* Prospero know what was happening in a completely different part of the island? It is this kind of juncture in the play which makes it necessary for the spectator to make a leap out of the literal mode into the metaphorical, symbolic one which is ruled by the imagination. And it was not necessarily any easier for Jacobean audiences to do this than for us today. Shakespeare's genius is revealed in the way he could address the outer and the inner in the same breath — as in the masterly fashion he has Prospero forgive Antonio. The "No" comes as an affirmation of his earlier remark (that he would "tell no tales"), by the way; though, simultaneously, it is a negation of the accusation Sebastian has just made.

> *Pros.*   No.
> For you, most wicked sir, whom to call brother
> Would even infect my mouth, I do forgive
> Thy rankest fault, — all of them; and require
> My dukedom of thee, which perforce, I know,
> Thou must restore.
>
>   (V.i.129-134)

Antonio is at last confronted. And it is no easy task, either, for Prospero to forgive him. The struggle is obvious. Yet, he *does* — and not mechanically, superficially, hypocritically — without mincing his words. This forgiveness has only emerged as a conscious attitude because of the recognition of the 'Antonio' within. As Marie-Louise von Franz says, "The individuation process . . . is incompatible with any sort of social power claim."[27]

Antonio does not reply. In fact, he says no more for the remainder of the play, except at V.i.256 where he mocks Caliban. His silence, more than anything, is a hermetic clue to his shadowy nature. We can never be sure that the Shadow has been defeated in its tendency to maintain an autonomous, evil existence. Or does Antonio's silence reflect an inner capitulation and integration? Jung was himself very clear on the difficulty of total assimilation.

> Although, with insight and good will, the shadow can to some extent
> be assimilated into the conscious personality, experience shows that there
> are certain features which offer the most obstinate resistance to moral

control and prove almost impossible to influence. These resistances are usually bound up with *projections*, which are not recognized as such, and their recognition is a moral achievement beyond the ordinary.

(CW.9.ii.p.9)

6. Look Down, You Gods And on This Couple Drop a Blessed Crown!

33. **Join brother and sister, & hand them the cup with the love potion.**

The ending of *The Tempest* resembles the swelling music of jubilation and many-voiced, contrapuntal, interwoven song which occurs in key points of integration in an opera by Mozart. And, what better expression of individuation! Each character, unihibitedly singing their own song, yet simultaneously in harmony with all the rest — so that what could be a cacophony of unrelated, warring voices becomes an ecstatic unity, transcending differences and allowing the fullest expression of individuality-in-relationship.

The stage at the end of *The Tempest* is dominated by Prospero — and yet (especially with good direction and intelligent acting) the others can all make themselves heard. For this play, perhaps more than all the rest, is a celebration of the project which Jung termed 'individuation'. Thus, all the characters should be strong and very much themselves — each should have his own distinct voice. It is all very well to see the various characters, as I have done in this book, as aspects of the psyche of the magus-shaman, in order to enrich the enjoyment of the play and to explore its hidden depths, but in a production, one wants each colour to sing out with a vigour all its own. This means going to the essence of each character and bringing out its particular vibration.

Alonso, for example, is very much the bereaved father and despairing king. The 'loss' of Ferdinand is a blow he can hardly bear. He can think of nothing else.

> *Alon.*   If thou be'st Prospero,
> Give us particulars of thy preservation;
> How thou hast met us here, whom three hours since
> Were wrack'd upon this shore; where I have lost —
> How sharp the point of this remembrance is! —
> My dear son Ferdinand.
>
> *Pros.*   I am woe for't, sir.
>
> *Alon.*   Irreparable is the loss; and patience
> Says it is past her cure.
>
> *Pros.*   I rather think
> You have not sought her help, of whose soft grace
> For the like loss I have her sovereign aid,
> And rest myself content.
>
>   (V.i.134-144)

There is a fascinating ambiguity in line 142 of Prospero's reply. Either Prospero is claiming that Alonso has not *sought* the help of "patience" or he is implying that the king has not sought the help of some other *feminine* being (i.e., "I rather think/ You have not sought *her* help."). If the latter, he may be referring, in fact, to Miranda herself — or to an unnamed divinity. In any case, the point is made: Alonso has not sought help from the feminine.

Prospero continues to play on the word, 'loss', in his next exchange with Alonso, sharing with the audience the knowledge which Alonso does not yet have: that Prospero has 'lost' his daughter to Ferdinand in the same fashion as Ferdinand is actually 'lost' to Alonso. Alonso is totally unaware of the real meaning behind Prospero's words.

> *Alon.*   You the like loss!
>
> *Pros.*   As great to me, as late; and, supportable
> To make the dear loss, have I means much weaker
> Than you may call to comfort you, for I
> Have lost my daughter.
>
> *Alon.*   A daughter?
> O heavens, that they were living both in Naples,
> The King and Queen there! that they were, I wish
> Myself were mudded in that oozy bed
> Where my son lies. When did you lose your daughter?
>
> *Pros.*   In this last tempest . . .
>
>   (V.i.144-153)

The moment is now approaching when Prospero can openly introduce the royal couple, the alchemical *coniunctio*, as a reality — and demystify the King. It is worth noting that these events run synchronistically: the King's recovery of the truth and the 'discovery' of the royal pair.

> *Pros.*   . . . Welcome, sir;
> This cell's my court: here have I few attendants,
> And subjects none abroad: pray you, look in.
> My dukedom since you have given me again,
> I will requite you with as good a thing;
> At least bring forth a wonder, to content ye
> As much as me my dukedom.
>
> *Here* Prospero *discovers* Ferdinand *and* Miranda *playing chess.*
>   (V.i.165-171)

The *wonder* is the royal couple in Prospero's cell. Thus, we see that the marriage of opposites goes hand in hand with the processes of individuation, i.e., the confrontation with the Shadow, the acceptance and recognition of evil (the will to power) in oneself and the consequent capacity to forgive it in others, as well as the revaluing of devalued aspects of the self — the feminine and, of course, the inferior function(s). This last, however, is yet to come. Prospero must still make his peace with Caliban.

First, there is the joyful reunion of father and son (*senex et puer*) and the acceptance, for the King, of a *new loss* and a *new gain*. I think that the simple device of the chess game is brilliant. It has long been accepted that the game of chess is an analogue of the course of love between two lovers. And, as this play is not a *literal* love story only, the chess-game serves to underline the symbolic nature of the romance. What better way to emphasize the equality of the two components of the *coniunctio*? Of course, this does not exclude the literal level. As Frank Kermode points out:[28] "Chess-games between lovers are frequently represented on wedding-chests and mirror-cases, and there is a characteristic mirror-case in the Victoria and Albert Museum which depicts a lover and a lady at play in a tent; allowing for the costume it could be an illustration to *The Tempest*". Playing chess was a "general and valued liberty permitted to medieval lovers".[29]

The King was duly astonished at the wonder Prospero has brought forth; but Ferdinand shows surprisingly little emotion on seeing his father. The man has ceased to be the most important person in his life.

> *Alon.*   If this prove
> A vision of the island, one dear son
> Shall I twice lose.

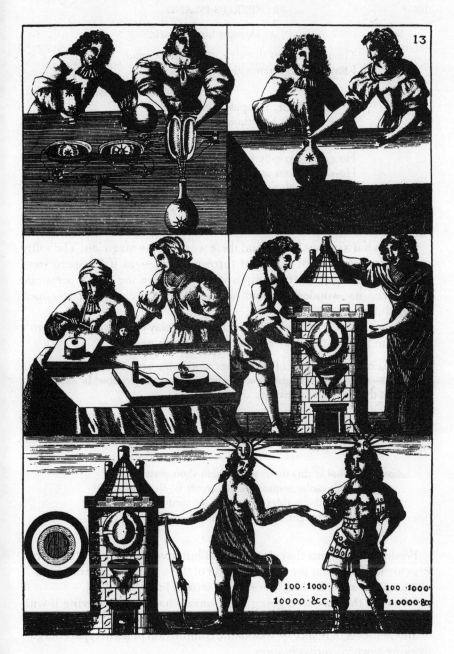

Seb.   A most high miracle!

Fer.   Though the seas threaten, they are merciful;
            I have curs'd them without cause.

Alon.   Now all the blessings
            Of a glad father compass thee about!
            Arise, and say how thou cam'st here.

Mir.   O, wonder!
            How many goodly creatures are there here!
            How beauteous mankind is! O brave new world,
            That has such people in't!

Pros.   'Tis new to thee.
                                          (V.i.175-184)

Oh — what a pathos lies behind these words of the magician! The softly spoken understatement is almost thrown away — as if Prospero were speaking to himself. Yet, through it, we perceive the soul's perennial innocence, its wonder and admiration ("Miranda") and its open vulnerability.

Herman Melville noticed it. In his copy of the play he encircled Prospero's answer and made this note at the bottom of the page: [30]

> Consider the character of the persons concerning whom Miranda says this — then Prospero's quiet words in comment — how terrible! In *Timon* itself there is nothing like it.

Ferdinand's father, however, is awestruck by the sight of Miranda. This was the last thing, we could imagine, he expected to see: his son playing chess with a 'goddess'.

Alon.   What is this maid with whom thou wast at play?
            Your eld'st acquaintance cannot be three hours:
            Is she the goddess that hath severed us,
            And brought us thus together?
                                          (V.i.185-188)

Ferdinand explains that she is mortal but given to him by "immortal Providence" and that she is the daughter of "this famous Duke of Milan", of whom, he says, he has "received a second life" (V.i.195).

While all this has been going on, Gonzalo has been observing it with great emotion. Finally, he speaks — and in his speech reveals an intuition of another level of reality — that of the conjunction of archetypal energies working towards individuation.

Gon.   I have inly wept,
Or should have spoke ere this. Look down, you gods,
And on this couple drop a blessed crown!
For it is you that have chalk'd forth the way
Which brought us hither.

Alon.   I say, Amen, Gonzalo!

Gon.   Was Milan thrust from Milan, that his issue
Should become Kings of Naples? O, rejoice
Beyond a common joy! and set it down
With gold on lasting pillars: in one voyage
Did Claribel her husband find at Tunis,
And Ferdinand, her brother, found a wife
Where he himself was lost, Prospero his dukedom
In a poor isle, and all of us ourselves
When no man was his own.

                                              (V.I.200-213)

And so, with these shiveringly beautiful words, Shakespeare tells us of
something beyond a common joy — something which he is struggling, yes
struggling, throughout the whole miraculous play to say: that, *deo concedente*,
there is a way for all of us to find ourselves when no man is his own. This
truth is so important that the bard has Gonzalo suggest setting it down "With
gold on lasting pillars" — which image will certainly stand forever in the
imagination of Western man.

7. As Strange a Maze as E'er Men Trod

35. The Sun & its shadow complete the work.

Who should appear now but the master and the bo'sun of the ship, "amazedly following" Ariel. Gonzalo is delighted and even reovers some of his former wit.

> (*Gon.*)   O, look, sir! here is more of us:
> I prophesied, if a gallows were on land,
> This fellow could not drown. Now, blasphemy,
> That swear'st grace o'erboard, not an oath on shore?
> Hast thou no mouth by land? What is the news?
>
> *Boats.*   The best news is, that we have safely found
> Our King, and company; the next, our ship —
> Which, but three glasses since, we gave out split —
> Is tight and yare and bravely rigg'd as when
> We first put out to sea.

The Master is the captain of the ship which has brought Prospero's enemies from the mainland. His silence, in contrast to that of the silenced Antonio, is symbolic of the silence of the greater forces (like the gods who have "chalk'd forth the way") moving within and behind this 'play'. The bo'sun says it all, anyway: how the ship is miraculously "tight and yare and bravely rigg'd" as when they first put out to sea. His words also underline the strict observance of time in *The Tempest*.

Ariel, in words inaudible to all but Prospero and ourselves, calls his master's attention to the service he has performed, and the magician acknoweldges him: "My tricksy spirit!" (V.i.226). We hear more of the, by no means meagre, capacity of Ariel to act as (spell) binder of souls, *Hermes katochos*, and as the escort of souls, *Hermes psychostolos*, in the boatswain's explanation to Alonso as to how he came to find the King and his company:

Boats.   . . . We were dead of sleep,
          And — how we know not — all clapp'd under hatches;
          Where, but even now, with strange and several noises
          Of roaring, shrieking, howling, jingling chains,
          And no diversity of sounds, all horrible,
          We were awak'd; straightway, at liberty;
          Where we, in all our trim, freshly beheld
          Our royal, good and gallant ship; our master
          Cap'ring to eye her: — on a trice, so please you,
          Even in a dream, were we divided from them,
          And were brought moping hither.

          ★

Alon.   This is as strange a maze as e'er men trod;
          And there is in this business more than nature
          Was ever conduct of: some oracle
          Must rectify our knowledge.

Pros.   Sir, my liege,
          Do not infest your mind with beating on
          The strangeness of this business; at pick'd leisure
          Which shall be shortly single, I'll resolve you,
          Which to you shall seem probable, of every
          These happen'd accidents; till when, be cheerful,
          And think of each thing well. (*Aside to Ari.*) Come
             hither, spirit:
          Set Caliban and his companions free;
          Untie the spell. (*Exit* Ariel). How fares my gracious sir?
          There are yet missing of your company
          Some few odd lads that you remember not.
                                        (V.i.230-255)

Moments later, Ariel returns, "driving Caliban, Stefano and Trinculo in their stolen apparel". At last, the circle is complete — for now, the last of the inferior elements are present. This is Shakespeare's genius: always to include the shadowy, low, grotesque, weak, miserable and foolish within the compass of humankind. The words he gives Stefano to speak are truly brilliant. The drunken butler utters the following profound thought — almost as if he spoke it unintentionally, as the result of a Bacchic confusion:

> *Ste.*   Every man shift for all the rest, and let no man take
> care for himself; for all is but fortune. — Coragio,
> bully-monster, coragio!
>
> (V.i.256-8)

Trinculo seems relieved to see the King and his company, but Caliban, catching sight of Prospero dressed as the Duke of Milan, is terrified:

> *Cal.*   O Setebos, these be brave spirits indeed!
> How fine my master is! I am afraid
> He will chastise me.
>
> (V.i.261-163)

Sebastian and Antonio exchange irrelevant remarks on the unhappy trio which has just flounced so unceremoniously onto the stage, but Prospero is quick to take control of the situation, explaining the collusion of the three men.

> *Pros.*   Mark but the badges of these men, my lords,
> Then say if they be true. This mis-shapen knave,
> His mother was a witch; and one so strong
> That could control the moon, make flows and ebbs,
> And deal in her command, without her power.
> These three have robb'd me; and this demi-devil —
> For he's a bastard one — had plotted with them
> To take my life. Two of these fellows you
> must know and own . . .
>
> (V.i.267-275)

The next seven words which Prospero speaks are certainly, for a follower of the path with a heart, among the most difficult and most necessary. I know of no other words in the corpus of Western literature which better express the nature of enlightenment:

> . . . this thing of darkness I
> Acknowledge mine.
>
> (V.i.275-6)

Whether it is an effort for Prospero to speak these words or not we do not know, but the effort which has brought him to the point where he can speak them at all has been considerable. Prospero finally sees himself in Caliban. And here we have an archetypal model for the process of individuation. To arrive at a meaningful spirituality and a state of wholeness, we must acknowledge our own darkness.

Neglecting to do this merely leads to a mock-wisdom, an empty goodness and a false sainthood. It is the embodiment of self-deception, ultimately sterile as spirit because it has rejected the moist ground of darkness which could give it sustenance. Spirit incarnates into the world by implanting itself in this darkness, taking root and bearing fruit for others. This, for me, is the fundamental message of the play. And it is extremely pertinent for our time. One could say that it was Shakespeare's message to the modern shamans of the Aquarian Age, his arcane transmission of insight to the newly-hatched adepts and mystics of the "brave new world" at the twentieth *fin de siècle*.

Caliban, of course, believes that Prospero means to lay some new torture on him, whining: "I shall be pinch'd to death." (V.i.276). The King's company recognizes Stefano and Trinculo, who are sorely abashed in the exposure of their drunken folly. Prospero demonstrates his universal awareness to them in a single comment: "You'ld be King o' the isle, sirrah?" (V.i.287). Stefano can only mumble a feeble reply. Prospero sends Caliban and his reeling friends into his cell, with the command — "as you look/ To have my pardon, trim it handsomely." (V.i.292-3). Caliban answers:

> *Cal.*   Ay, that I will; and I'll be wise hereafter,
> And seek for grace. What a thrice-double ass
> Was I, to take this drunkard for a god,
> And worship this dull fool!
>
> (V.i.294-297)

Thus, in his way even Caliban has learned something through his sorry debacle.

Prospero, majestically and regally, turns to King Alonso and warmly addresses him:

> *Pros.*   Sir, I invite your Highness and your train
> To my poor cell, where you shall take your rest
> For this one night; which, part of it, I'll waste
> With such discourse as, I no doubt, shall make it
> Go quick away: the story of my life,
> And the particular accidents gone by
> Since I came to this isle: and in the morn
> I'll bring you to your ship, and so to Naples,
> Where I have hope to see the nuptial
> Of these our dear-belov'd solemnized;
> And thence retire me to my Milan, where
> Every third thought shall be my grave.

> *Alon.*   I long
>   To hear the story of your life, which must
>   Take the ear strangely.
>
> *Pros.*   I'll deliver all;
>   And promise you calm seas, auspicious gales,
>   And sail so expeditious, that shall catch
>   Your royal fleet far off . . .
>
>   (V.i.300-16)

"The story of my life/ And the particular accidents gone by" — how human and how endearing. For even the greatest among us lives and breathes and shares a common destiny. Shakespeare has once again enriched our lives with a story, told with such passion and devotion to the spirit in man that one could almost believe that it was, in some deeply inner way, his own story.

David Grene in his book, "Reality and the Heroic Pattern", says that *The Tempest*'s ending "leaves one with the prevailing sense of melancholy and failure".[31] Melancholy certainly. But I feel that Grene is very far off the mark in his analysis of this melancholy. He is caught in his own father-complex, and his analysis is an expression of this. What he does not see is what Prospero is seeing when he says "Every third thought shall be my grave". Grene says, "What is left is the weariness of an old man who has no longer any passionate concern even with what is good and right in the new pattern of events to which he has lent his help. The doubleness of life in beauty and ugliness, the imperfection of consummation, the frailty of humanity, the terror of death's meaninglessness, are too much for him — as a person."[32]

Shakespeare obviously expected that many people would not understand him in this last play. Therefore, he wrote an epilogue in which Prospero comes back on stage after the play is over and asks the audience for help, for breath to fill his sails so that his project will not fail. Is he not asking us to use *our own* imagination, our creative spirit, to give life to his precious gift: a guiding myth for the journey towards wholeness?

Of course, the ending is sad. Although, outwardly, it is a 'happy ending' and the "nuptials of our dear-belov'd" will be celebrated and Prospero shall soon return to Milan, it is also the end of an era, the farewell to the island and the recognition of the finality which puts a full-stop to the projects of this lifetime — death. It also seems to be Shakespeare's farewell to the stage and perhaps to his active involvement with drama. It even has overtones of a greater, historical change — the fading of the Renaissance traditions of alchemy, hermeticism and the song of Ariel/Mercurius, the nightingale of the Imagination.

Pros.   (*Aside to Ariel*) My Ariel, chick,
        That is thy charge: then to the elements
        Be free, and fare thou well!

                                        (V.i.316-318)

Epilogue

Spoken by Prospero

Now my charms are all o'erthrown,
And what strength I have's mine own,
Which is most faint: now, 'tis true,
I must be here confin'd by you,
Or sent to Naples. Let me not.
Since I have my dukedom got,
And pardon'd the deceiver, dwell
In this bare island by your spell;
But release me from my bands
With the help of your good hands:
Gentle breath of yours my sails
Must fill, or else my project fails,
Which was to please. Now I want
Spirits to enforce, Art to enchant;
And my ending is despair,
Unless I be reliev'd by prayer,
Which pierces so, that it assaults
Mercy itself, and frees all faults.
   As you from crimes would pardon'd be,
   Let your indulgence set me free. *Exit*.

Ora
Lege Lege Lege Relege labora
et Invenies.

36.

Notes to Part III

1. C. G. Jung: CW 14, p. 501.
2. Ibid., p. 89.
3. Jung: CW 13, p. 250.
4. Robert Graves maintained that the play reflected Shakespeare's for-giveness of the pain caused him by his 'Dark Lady of the Sonnets' eloping with his 'master mistress', a young boy named Will or W.H. Personally, I take Graves's essay, *The Sources of The Tempest* (1925) to be a piece of mischief. Graves hints at a multiplicity of sources for the play, which he loosely combines in an ever-increasingly giddy spiral of different interpretations. He explains his view with this curious sentence: "He (Shakespeare) was the 'master poet' who insisted on his own 'absurd courses', and carried on something of a city-mystery tradition in which each guild contributed an episode of a topical or humorous kind strung on a loose thread of Scriptural history." See: R. Graves: *The Common Asphodel*. p. 27ff. Hamish Hamilton, London, 1949.
5. Edward Conze (ed.): *Buddhist Texts Through the Ages*. Harper & Row, N.Y., 1964, p. 161.
6. T. Looney: *Shakespeare Identified*. Vol. 1., p. 418. Kenikat Press, N.Y., 1975.
7. "When one speaks of a 'Bodhisattva', what dharma does that word 'Bodhisattva' denote? I do not, O Lord, see that dharma, 'Bodhisattva', nor a dharma called 'perfect wisdom'. Since I neither find, nor apprehend, nor see a dharma, 'Bodhisattva', nor a 'perfect wisdom', what Bodhisattva shall I instruct and admonish in what perfect wisdom? And yet, O Lord, if, when this is pointed out, a Bodhisattva's heart does not become cowed, nor stolid, does not despair nor despond, if he does not turn away or become dejected, does not tremble, is not frightened or terrified, it is just this Bodhisattva, this great being, who

should be instructed in perfect wisdom.'' — from opening lines of *The Astasahasrika Prajnaparamita Sutra*, transl. by E. Conze as *The Perfection of Wisdom — in 8,000 slokas*. Asiatic Society, Calcutta, 1958.

8. Ibid., p. 69.

9. As quoted in K. Venkata Ramanan: *Nagarjuna's Philosophy*. Bharatiya Vidya Prakashan, Varansi, India, 1971.

10. Ibid., p. 161.

11. C. G. Jung: CW 16, p. 314.

12. C. G. Jung: CW 16, p. 313.

13. *Astasahasrika Prajnaparamita*. p. 18.

14. C. G. Jung: CW 13, p. 237.

15. C. G. Jung: CW 11, p. 578-9.

16. C. G. Jung: CW 16, p. 319.

17. *The Tempest*. Arden edition. Kermode's footnotes to V.i.1-5.

18. Dover Wilson: *The Meaning of The Tempest*, publ. by The Literary and Philosophical Society of Newcastle Upon Tyne, 1936, p. 17.

19. Hillman: *Revisioning Psychology*, p. x.

20. Ibid.

21. Three other great unsolved mysteries of the play are:

    (1) What did Sycorax do so that they would not take her life?

    (2) To what astrological/astronomical situation is Prospero referring by 'my zenith doth depend upon/ a most auspicious star, whose influence/ If now I court not, but omit, my fortunes/ Will ever after droop''? and

    (3) By what means does Prospero raise the storm?

    I feel that (2) is the most accessible of the mysteries, but I hardly dare suggest the solution which I feel harmonizes best with this interpretation. It would, textually and alchemically speaking, be most appropriate with a conjunction of the Sun and Moon. Dramatically, this would present problems, as it would mean, most likely, an eclipse of the sun. This could easily happen within the given four hour period, but it could also imply a period of total darkness between 4 to 7 minutes on stage. (Information obtained from the Royal Astronomical Society.) One possibility could be a symbolic period of darkness, say from IV.i.139-160 Prospero's dreamspeech.

22. Appendix D. *The Tempest*. Arden edition.

23. Kerenyi: *Goddesses*. p. 33.

24. D. G. James: *The Dream of Prospero*. Clarendon Press, Oxford, 1967.

25. Ibid., p. 68.

26. cf. William Blake's words on the same subject in *Milton*, Plate 28: ''For in this Period the Poet's Work is Done, and all the Great

Events of Time start forth & are conceiv'd in such a Period,
Within a Moment, a Pulsation of the Artery.''

27. Marie-Louise von Franz: *C. G. Jung — His Myth in Our Time*. Little, Brown & Co., Boston, Toronto, 1975, p. 263.

28. F. Kermode: Arden edition of *The Tempest* (*op. cit.*), p. 123 note to this scene.

29. Ibid.

30. Quoted in Charles Olson's: *Call Me Ismael*. City Lights, Calif., 1947.

31. David Grene: *Reality and the Heroic Pattern*. The Univ. of Chic. Press, Chicago & London, 1967, p. 100.

32. Ibid.

Appendix I

Some dates relevant to a discussion of Shakespeare's *The Tempest*.

1460 — Marsilio Ficino's translation of the *Corpus hermeticum* (by order of Cosimo de' Medici).

1471 — George Ripley (English Alchemist) writes *The Compound of Alchemy*.

1484 — The *Bull* of Pope Innocent VIII against witchcraft written, thus creating the Holy Office of the Inquisition.

1486 — First edition of the inquisitional manual, *Malleus Maleficarum* in Germany.

1489 — Ficino: *On Drawing Down the Life of Heaven*.

1490 — George Ripley dies.

1493 — Philippus Aureolus Theophrastus Bombastus von Hohenheim (Paracelsus) born.

1527 — John Dee born.

1533 — Birth of (Queen) Elizabeth I to Anne Boleyn and Henry VIII.
    — Cornelius Agrippa: *De Occulta Philosophia*.

1537 — Paracelsus: *De Natura Rerum*.

1541 — Paracelsus dies.

1558 — Elizabeth accedes to the English throne, becoming Queen Elizabeth I.

1564 — William Shakespeare born.

1566 — Michael Maier born.

1574 — Robert Fludd born.

1583 — Giordano Bruno visits England.

1584 — John Dee and Edward Kelly travel to Bohemia. Dee makes a bid to become Rudolph II's Court Philosopher. Possible meeting between Dee and Maier, then court physician to Rudolph.

1584 — Reginald Scot: *Discoverie of Witchcraft*.

1585 — Bruno: *De Gli Eroici Furori* published in England.

1588 — The Spanish Armada. Bruno in Prague.

1589 — Dee returns to England from Prague.

— First edition of Paracelusus' *Complete Works*.

1590/92 — Trials of the North Berwick witches and beginning of great persecution of witches in England.

1591 — Ripley's *The Compound of Alchemy* first published. Dee's *Monas* reprinted.

Early 1590's — Shakespeare: *Two Gentlemen of Verona, The Taming of the Shrew, Romeo and Juliet, Henry VI, pts. 1, 2, & 3, Richard III, Love's Labour's Lost, The Comedy of Errors, A Midsummer Night's Dream.*

1594 — *The Pearle of Practice* — A Collection of John Hester's Chemical Recipes. Published by Forester.

1597 — *Demonologie* by King James VI of Scotland, later King James I of England.

1599 — Lambsprink: *De Lapide Philosophico* (alchemical text).

— Basil Valentinus: *The Twelve Keys* (alchemical text). Germany.

— Opening of the Globe Theatre.

Late 1590's — Shakespeare: *The Merchant of Venice, Henry IV, pts. 1 & 2, The Merry Wives of Windsor, Much Ado About Nothing, Henry V, Julius Caesar.*

1600 — Giordano Bruno burnt at the stake in Rome.

1601 — Campanella imprisoned in Naples.

1602 — *Theatrum Chemicum* (alchemical texts) edited by Lazarus Zetzner. Ober-Ursel.

— Lost early version of *Chymische Hochzeit* by Johann Valentin Andrea.

Early 1600's — Shakespeare: *As You Like It, Twelfth Night, Hamlet, Troilus and Cressida, All's Well That End's Well, Othello, Measure for Measure.*

1603 — Queen Elizabeth dies. James I accedes to the throne.

1603 — Florio's translation of Montaigne's essay, *Of the Caniballes*.

1604 — Sendivogus: *Novum Lumen Chemicum* (alchemical text). Prague.

— John Dowland: *Lachrimae or Seven Teares figured in Seven Pavans*. A piece for lute and viols.

1605 — Thomas Tymme: *The Practice of Chymicall & Hermeticall Physicke*.

1606/7 — Shakespeare: *Anthony and Cleopatra.*

1607/8 — Shakespeare: *King Lear, Timon of Athens, Coriolanus, Pericles.*

1609/10 — Shakespeare: *Cymbeline.*

1610 — Sylvester Jourdaine: *Discoverie of the Bermudas.*

1611 — On Hallowmass or All Saints' Day, November 1st, *The Tempest* given as a command performance by the King's Majesty's Servants at the banqueting house in Whitehall.

— Shakespeare: *The Winter's Tale.*

1612 — Prince Henry dies. Rudolph II abdicates to his brother, Mathias, and dies within the year. Michael Meyer in England.

— *The Tempest* performed for the court and especially for Princess Elizabeth and her betrothed, Prince Frederick of Bohemia, the Elector Palatinate, December 26.

1613 — February 14 — Elizabeth and Frederick married in England.

— Frederick and Elizabeth installed in the castle in Heidelberg.

— Shakespeare's Henry VIII first performed.

1616 — Shakespeare's daughter, Judith, married.

— Publication of *The Chemical Wedding of Christian Rosencreutz* with Dee's 'monas' on the title page.

— April 23 — William Shakespeare dies on 52nd birthday.

1617 — *Atlanta Fugiens* (set of 50 alchemical engravings) published by Michael Maier.

1619 — On August 26 the Bohemians offer the crown of Bohemia to Frederick.

1619-1620 — Reign of The Winter King and Queen of Bohemia (Frederick and Elizabeth).

1620 — November 8th: Complete defeat of Frederick's troops in battle of White Mountain. Catholic (Hapsburg) conquest of Bohemia and the Palatinate. Frederick & Elizabeth flee to the Hague. Thirty Years' War rages.

— The worst of all the witch persecutions begins.

1622 — Michael Maier disappears in Magdeburg.

1623 — Mersenne publishes first attack on Renaissance Magia (Ficino, Pico, Agrippa etc.) and begins attack on Robert Fludd and his work.

— Descartes shows himself to friends in Paris to demonstrate that he is not invisible and therefore not a 'Rosicrucian'.

1632 — Death of Elector Frederick, 'Winter King of Bohemia'.

1633 — Trial of Galileo.

1644 — Descartes publishes the 'Principia', establishing the basis for Cartesian mechanism.

Appendix II
List of Plates

1. *Atalanta Fugiens* (Michael Maier, 1612), emblem **XXX**.

   O, Sun you do not achieve anything alone, if I am not present with my
   forces,
   Just as the cock is useless without the help of the hen.
   And in my turn I, the moon, want your help,
   Just as the cock is desired by the hen.
   Foolish is he who would want to free from the bonds those things
   From which nature urgently requires that they are united.

2. *Mutus Liber*, 1677, plate 1. Title page, showing trumpeting angels on
   'Jacob's Ladder', summoning the sleeping alchemist.
3. Portrait of James I of England by John de Critz (?) (1610). Reproduced
   by permission of the National Maritime Museum, London.
4. Portrait of John Dee (1594) — Anon. Reproduced by permission of
   the Ashmolean Museum, Oxford.
5. *Mutus Liber*, plate 2. The alchemist and his mystica soror kneel in an
   attitude of humility before the vessel of transformation, symbolising
   the *opus*. Above them two angels display an image of the first stage of
   the work.
6. *Atalanta Fugiens*, emblem I.

   When the unborn child, which lies hidden in the womb of the North
   wind,
   One day will rise to the light, alive,
   He alone will be able to surpass all deeds of heroism
   With his art, his hand, bodily strength and spirit,
   Let him not be born for you like a Coeso, and not as a useless
   abortion,
   Not as an Agrippa, but under a lucky star.

7. *Atalanta Fugiens*, emblem XXXI.

> The king, on whose head the crown pressed heavily,
>> Swims in the wide sea, and continually calls in a loud voice:
> Why do you not come to my rescue? Why do you not all rush forward,
>> You, whom I can make happy, once I am saved from the waters?
> Take me back to my realm, if you are sensible,
>> And no poverty nor any bodily disease will vex you any more.

8. *Atalanta Fugiens*, emblem XIX.

> Twice two brothers are standing in a long row,
>> One of whom holds a lump of earth in his hand and a second one carries water.
> The share of the others is air and fire.
>> If you want them to perish, kill only one of them,
> And all will extirpated by the murder of their relative,
>> Because mutual bonds of nature united them.

9. Alchemical library and laboratory from *Tripus Aureus* by Michael Maier, 1677. The winged dragon in the retort symbolises the unity of the opposites.

10. *Atalanta Fugiens*, emblem X.

> The entire Machina Mundi, riveted together, depends on this chain,
>> That everything alike rejoices in the like:
> In this way, Mercury is connected with Mercury, and fire with fire.
>> May this be given to you as the ultimate object for your art,
> Vulcan sets Hermes in motion, but the winged Hermes
>> Dissolves you, O Cynthia, but she, your sister, decomposes you, O Apollo. ·

11. *Atalanta Fugiens*, emblem II.

> Romulus is said to have been nursed at the coarse udders of a wolf,
>> But Jupiter to have been nursed by a goat, and these facts are said to be believed.
> Should we then wonder if we assert
>> That the earth suckles the tender Child of the Philosophers with its milk?
> If an insignificant animal nursed such great heroes,
>> Shall he not be great, who has the Territorial Globe as a nurse.

12. *Atalanta Fugiens*, emblem III.

> Let not he who loves scrutinising secret dogmas
>> Neglect to take as an example everything which can help him.

Don't you see how a woman is accustomed to cleaning dirty laundry
  By pouring hot water over it?
Follow her example, so that you will not fail in your art,
  For the water washes the precipitation of the black body away.

13. *Atalanta Fugiens*, emblem XXXII.

A moist plant, living under the waves of the sea near Sicily,
  Multiplied its branches in the tepid water.
That plant is called Coral, and gets harder,
  When Boreas sends frost from the cold North.
It becomes stone, with many ramifications and has a red colour:
  This is a suitable image for the Stone of Nature.

14. *Mutus Liber*, plate 3. Birds with wings outspread show that the work has begun. Left-hand connections unite the adepts to their contrasexual aspects in the depths of the sea.
15. *Mutus Liber*, plate 4. Between the figures of a sheep and a bull, the adepts have collected 'dew' or the quintessence of five 'beds' or elemental matrices.
16. *Mutus Liber*, plate 5. Distillation of the essence. *Coagulatio*. The appearance of the moon and the divine child in the laboratory.
17. *Atalanta Fugiens*, emblem XXVII.

The Rose Garden of Wisdom has an abundance of various flowers
  But the gate is always closed with strong bolts;
Only one thing of little value is found in the world which is the
    key to it.
  Without this key you will walk like somebody without legs,
You will try in vain to climb up to the steep top of the Parnassus,
  You, who have hardly enough strength to remain standing on
    flat ground.

18. *Mutus Liber*, plate 6. Further distillations. The appearance of the sun, the flower and the strung solar bow in the laboratory.
19. *Mutus Liber*, plate 7. *Solutio*. Transformation through great heat. *Calcinatio*. The appearance of the puer-senex duo and the sword.
20. *Atalanta Fugiens*, emblem XXIV.

Make sure that you catch the voracious wolf,
  By throwing the king's body before it, that it may satisfy its
    voracity with it.
Then throw it on the pile, where Vulcan kindles the fire,
  That through this the monster may be reduced to ashes.
Do this time after time, and so the king will rise from death,

And he will be proud of his Lion's heart.

21. *Atalanta Fugiens*, emblem **XLVII**.

The Wolf comes from the place where the Sun rises,
But from where the Sun sinks into the Sea, the Dog comes,
in raging fury;
The one bites the other, and the other bites back, in a torturous rage,
They were both seen furious, with their muzzles wide open.
They are the stones belonging to each other, which are given away for
nothing,
Everywhere, to all, at all times; may you understand them.

22. *Atalanta Fugiens*, emblem **XXI**.

Make a circle out of a man and a woman,
From which a quadrangular body arises with equal sides.
Derive from it a triangle, which is in contact on all sides with a
round sphere,
Then the Stone will have come into existence.
If such a great thing is not immediately in your mind,
Then know that you will understand everything, if you understand
the theory of Geometry.

23. *Atalanta Fugiens*, emblem **XXXIV**.

The bath shines because of the conception of the child, and the sky
because of his birth,
And after that, red, he strides over the waters,
And he becomes white on top of the mountains,
He who continually remains the sole care of scientists.
He is a stone and he is not a stone, and when somebody possesses this
noble gift of heaven,
By a present of God, he will be happy.

24. *Atalanta Fugiens*, emblem **XXVIII**.

King Duench, shining with the weapons of the Green Lion,
Swollen by bile, was horrible in his behaviour.
Thereupon he sends for the physician Pharut.
The latter promises him health and has a steam-bath prepared,
Herein he bathes and bathes again, under the glass arch,
Till, by the wet dew, he is freed from all bile.

25. *Atalanta Fugiens*, emblem **XXV**.

It is no insignificant work of art, to kill the Dragon in such a way
That it does not crawl along the ground, soon revived.

Its own brother and sister together smash its head with a club,
   And nothing else can bring it down.
Phoebus is its brother, and Cynthia its sister;
   The Python was felled by his hand, Orion by hers.

26. *Mutus Liber*, plate 10. *Coniunctio* of the moon-star and sun-flower in the alembic. Marriage of opposites, symbolized by personified sun and moon holding hands.

27. *Atalanta Fugiens*, emblem XXXVIII.

In Antiquity they called a twofold being Rebis,
   Because it is man and woman in one body, the Hermaphrodite,
For it is said that the Hermaphrodite is born on two mountains,
   To whom the all-feeding Venus gave birth for Hermes.
Do not despise the bisexual being,
   For man as well as woman, who together are one and the same,
      will give birth to the King for you.

28. *Atalanta Fugiens*, emblem XLVI.

Jupiter sent a couple of eagles from Delphi,
   As is said, to the regions of sunrise and sunset,
While he desires to investigate into the centre of the Earth.
   These eagles return simultaneously to Delphi, according to the
      legend,
But they are two stones belonging together, which meet in the right way,
   The one from the East, the other from the West.

29. *Atalanta Fugiens*, emblem XXXVII.

Three things from the foundation of the mastership:
   Stinking water, snow-white vapour, and a Lion with a green fur.
Like a mother, the water produces the other elements
   And for the wise it is the last and the first factor in the making
      of the stone.
But the ore of Hermes is the green Lion,
   And the stone, known from the chapters of the books, is white
      smoke and water.

30. *Atalanta Fugiens*, emblem XIV.

An atrocious hunger taught the Polyps to gnaw at their own legs,
   And taught men to feed on human flesh.
Now the dragon, while it bites itself in its tail and devours it,
   For the most part itself, becomes food for itself.
This dragon will have to be conquered, by the sword, hunger and
      imprisonment,

Till it devours itself and spits itself out, kills itself and
generates itself again.

31. *Mutus Liber*, plate 11. Final phase of the *opus*. Appearance of four windows
in the laboratory indicating completion or wholeness. Appearance of
the zodiacal sign of Libra in connection with the *coniunctio*.

32. *Atalanta Fugiens*, emblem XLVIII.

The king of the spring, powerful on account of his wealth and
peoples, liked water,
Which was brought to him by his servants, at his order.
He drank and drank again and soon his veins were saturated with it,
And he, gaily-coloured, was caught by famous physicians.
After they had purified him by letting him sweat, purge and vomit
Both his cheeks were soon coloured rose-red.

33. *Atalanta Fugiens*, emblem IV.

The human race would not be so numerous now in the world,
If not, as first wife, the sister had been given to the brother,
So join two descendants of one pair of parents with confidence,
That they may live in marriage as husband and wife.
Drink to each of them from the cup with the sweet love potion,
And their love will raise the hope of a fruit.

34. *Mutus Liber*, plate 13. *Circulatio* as applied to the *coniunctio* of plate 10.
This time there is an evident increase in the value of the result — from
10 we have gone to 100, 1,000 and 10,000, symbolizing the *multiplicatio*
of the final fruition of the *opus*.

35. *Atalanta Fugiens*, emblem XLV.

The Sun, the bright torch of Heaven, does not penetrate dense bodies,
That is why there remains shadow on the parts turned away from it.
Although the shadow is the most insignificant of all things,
It has been of much use to the Astronomers,
But Sol and its shadow give more gifts to the Philosophers
Because it means the completion of the art of making gold.

36. *Mutus Liber*, plate 14. The summing up of the *opus*. Images of the tools
needed for the work and the care required — symbolized by the thrice
repeated image of the tongs (in band two) and the balances, mortar
and crucibles (in band three). The bottom band indicates the great
secrecy attached to the work and the central importance of Mercury.
(The mystica soror is perhaps indicating with her right hand that the
process shown above her is a mistake — the liquid poured from the
cup seems to be missing the container.) The words are an injunction

to the reader to ''Pray, read, read, read and read again, work and you will succeed.''

37. *Mutus Liber*, plate 15. The ascension of the senex in a jubilant quaternio over the supine form of ego consciousness, symbolized by Heracles with club and lion-skin.

Bibliography

R. Bernheimer: *Wild Men in the Middle Ages*. Harvard University Press, 1952.

Marsilio Ficino: *The Book of Life* (Liber de Vita) translated by Charles Boer. Spring Publications, Dallas, 1980.

Peter French: *John Dee — The World of an Elizabethan Magus*. Routledge and Kegan Paul, London, 1972.

Joscelyn Godwin: *Robert Fludd*. Thames & Hudson, London, 1979.

Robert Graves: *Greek Myths*. Vols. 1 & 2. Penguin, London, 1955.

Robert Graves: *The White Goddess*. Faber & Faber, London, 1971.

James Hillman: *Anima I & Anima II* in *Spring* (journal) 1973 and 1974. Spring Publications, Dallas.

J. Hillman: *The Myth of Analysis*. Harper Colophon, Harper & Row, N.Y., London, 1972.

J. Hillman: *The Negative Senex and a Renaissance Solution* in *Spring 1976*. Spring Publications, Dallas.

J. Hillman et al: *Puer Papers*. Spring Publications, Dallas, 1979.

J. Hillman: *Revisioning Psychology*. Harper, N.Y. & London, 1975.

King James I (VI of Scotland): *Daemonology* (1597).

King James I. *Newes From Scotland* (1591).

Ben Jonson: *The Alchemist*. Penguin edition, London, 1978.

C. G. Jung: Collected Works: Vol. 6 — *Psychological Types*; Vol. 9, Part 1 — *The Archetypes and the Collective Unconscious*; Vol. 9, Part 2 — *Aion*; Vol. 11 — *Psychology and Religion: West and East*; Vol. 13 — *Alchemical Studies*; Vol. 14 — *Mysterium Coniunctionis*; Vol. 16: *The Practice of Psychotherapy*. Translated by R. F. C. Hull, Routledge and Kegan Paul, London.

C. G. Jung: *Letters*. ed. by G. Adler. Routledge and Kegan Paul, London, 1973.

C. G. Jung: *Man and His Symbols*. Aldus Books, London, 1964.

C. G. Jung: *Psychological Commentary on Kundalini Yoga. Lecture 1. Spring 1975.* Spring Publications, Dallas.

Carl Kerenyi: *Dionysos.* Translated by Ralph Manheim. Routledge and Kegan Paul, London, 1976.

C. Kerenyi: *Goddesses of Sun and Moon.* Translated by Murray Stein. Spring Publications, Dallas, 1979.

C. Kerenyi: *Hermes — Guide of Souls.* Translated by Murray Stein. Spring Publications, 1976.

G. Wilson Knight: *The Crown of Life.* Methuen & Co., London, 1947.

Heinrich Kramer and James Sprenger: *Malleus Malificarum* (The Hammer of Witches). Translated by Montague Summers. Arrow Books, 1971.

Martin Lings: *Shakespeare in the Light of Sacred Art.* Allen & Unwin, London, 1966.

Barry Lopez: *Of Wolves and Men.* J. M. Dent & Sons, London, 1978.

Rafael Lopez-Pedraza: *Hermes and His Children.* Spring Publications, Zurich, 1977.

W. F. Otto: *The Homeric Gods.* Translated by Moses Hadas. Thames & Hudson, London, 1954.

K. Venkata Ramanan: *Nagarjuna's Philosophy.* Bharitiya Vidya Prakashan. Varanasi, India, 1971.

William Shakespeare: *The Tempest.* Arden Edition. Editor Frank Kermode. Methuen, London, 1979.

C. J. Sisson: *The Magic of Prospero* in *Shakespeare Survey. Vol. 11.* Cambridge, 1958.

R. Stein: *Incest and Human Love.* Penguin Books Maryland (USA), 1974.

Colin Still: *The Timeless Theme.* Ivor Nicolson & Watson, London, 1936.

Virgil: *Aeneid.* Translated by W. F. Jackson Knight. Penguin, London, 1956.

Laurens Van Der Post: *Religion and the Renewal of Man and His Societies.* (Printed talk). Wesminster Pastoral Foundation, 23 Kensington Square, London W8, 1979.

Marie-Louise von Franz: *A Psychological Interpretation of The Golden Ass of Apuleius.* Spring Publications, Zurich, 1970.

Marie-Louise von Franz: *C. G. Jung — His Myth in Our Time.* Little, Brown & Co., Boston, 1975.

Marie-Louise von Franz: *Interpretation of Fairy Tales.* Spring Publications, 1978.

Marie-Louise von Franz and James Hillman: *Jung's Typology.* Spring Publications, 1971.

Marie-Louise von Franz: *Shadow and Evil in Fairy Tales.* Spring Publications, 1974.

D. P. Walker: *Spiritual and Demonic Magic from Ficino to Campanella.* The

University of Nôtre Dame, Paris, 1975. (The Warburg Institute, University of London, 1958).

Dover Wilson: *The Meaning of The Tempest*. The Literary and Philosophical Society of Newcastle Upon Tyne, 1936.

Frances Yates: *Giordano Bruno and the Hermetic Tradition*. Routledge and Kegan Paul, London, 1964.

Frances Yates: *The Occult Philosophy in the Elizabethan Age*. Routledge and Kegan Paul, London, 1979.

Frances Yates: *The Rosicrucian Enlightenment*. Routledge and Kegan Paul, 1972.

Frances Yates: *Shakespeare's Last Plays*. Routledge and Kegan Paul, 1975.

Heinrich Zimmer: *The King and the Corpse*. Bollingen, Washington D.C., 1948.

Index

37.